LIFE WITH SCARS

A RARE CASES PUBLICATION

ISBN: 978-0-9963697-0-1

Printed in the USA

Note: The stories contained within this course are based on true accounts. Only names of persons and inconsequential details have been modified to retain anonymity.

Rare Cases LLC
www.RareCases.com

Book cover photograph and design: Clayton Hall
Workbook interior design: Jean Boles

presents

LIFE WITH SCARS

A Guide to Emotionally Overcoming Physical Trauma
With Mentor and Consultant

Brady Armstrong

CONTENTS

5 DEDICATION

7 ABOUT THE AUTHOR

9 FOREWORD

11 INTRODUCTION

15 OVERVIEW

17 BACKGROUND

23 THE CHALLENGE

27 FOUR FORCES

81 THE PRIVATE SECTOR

89 THE PUBLIC SECTOR

103 HOME AND FAMILY LIFE

111 SOCIAL LIFE AND FRIENDSHIPS

123 LIFE AT SCHOOL

140 LIFE AT WORK

156 A ROMANTIC LIFE

173 Photography Credits

DEDICATION

This book is dedicated to anyone who is currently struggling with his or her physical appearance, to the many, like me, who have struggled and have overcome, and to anyone else who wants to understand how and why this struggle exists.

ABOUT THE AUTHOR

Brady Armstrong is a distinguished author, mentor, philanthropist, speaker and is the founder of Rare Cases LLC. For over a decade Brady has been empowering people to effectively govern their personal lives by overcoming physical and emotional trauma. His authored works and presentations have been acclaimed by American and international audiences. By combining empathy, personal experience and enthusiasm he communicates compelling principles that incite lasting personal change.

At the age of six, Brady's extraordinarily rare case of chickenpox received its first public spotlight on television by the CBS News affiliate KFMB in San Diego, CA in 1992. His subsequent emotional and social dealings of living with scars and of growing up while "looking different" have been documented and published for global application in the workbook *Life with Scars*, which provides practical and pragmatic lessons and anecdotes for others to learn from. Through its website, Rare Cases offers additional resources and tools for trauma survivors of diverse backgrounds.

Brady is a husband and father of two children and counting. He and his family currently reside in Phoenix, Arizona.

FOREWORD

Brady Armstrong has set up Rare Cases but he's also written a rare thing in today's internet online world – a hard-copy workbook no less that anyone who is trying to come to terms with living with scarring to their face or body or who looks unusual for any other reason will find very valuable.

The idea of a workbook to learn a foreign language is familiar enough; what Brady has done is to reflect on his experience and that of others to create a 'life skills course' for living with scars. It's full of great advice, smart analogies and tough lessons gently told. He makes clear that working through the lessons will take time as will the advice to really percolate through your life so that, for example, "the people closest to you need to have a sound understanding that you are not a victim of your scars'. But it will be time well spent.

His own experience shines strongly throughout the course – and his enthusiasm for life is infectious. His workbook is above all about taking control of your life – easily said but with his guidance, much more doable. Read on...

James Partridge
Founder and Chief Executive, Changing Faces
www.changingfaces.org.uk

Changing Faces is the leading charity in the UK supporting and representing people with conditions, marks and scars that affect their appearance. Find their online self-help guides at https://www.changingfaces.org.uk/Adults

INTRODUCTION

Welcome to Rare Cases, where anyone challenged with scars and disfigurement can gain resilience and success! Adapting to a life with scars or disfigurement can be a long and painful process. This course is not only designed to assist you in adapting to the challenges quickly, but also with developing the ability to thrive long term.

Trauma comes to all of us with major setbacks. If you desire fulfillment in your personal and social life, then completely overcoming the challenges that scars and disfigurement unavoidably bring is the key to being able to move forward. I invite you to put the lessons within this program to work. Once complete, refer back to them and repeat as often as necessary.

With the **Rare Cases Life With Scars** program, your confidence will increase, and over time you will feel comfortable and competent in more situations than you thought possible. Consider yourself on the path to excellence. You are a *rare case*, and you will soon discover how your differences actually make you strong!

There is so much potential for someone with a story like yours and this is the perfect place to gain access to that potential.

I can't wait to get started!

Brady Armstrong
Founder, Rare Cases

Dear reader,

This course will instruct you to make important decisions about the way you live your life. Here you will be encouraged to analyze the way you react in different situations and perhaps to form new opinions about life. To these instructions many will say, "It's easier said than done," and they are absolutely right.

As a mentor, please don't think of me as being on the horse, holding the reins, and taking you to where you need to be. Instead, see me as though I were standing on the path in front of you, at the fork in the road and pointing in each direction saying, "If you continue on this way, you'll end up falling off a rocky cliff. Alternatively, if you go that way you'll head straight for the banquet. I know, because I've been down this path before."

As you go into this course, remember, you are the one holding the reins. You can take my words, coming from someone with experience, and act on them, or choose not to. Ultimately, it is you who decides which way to go.

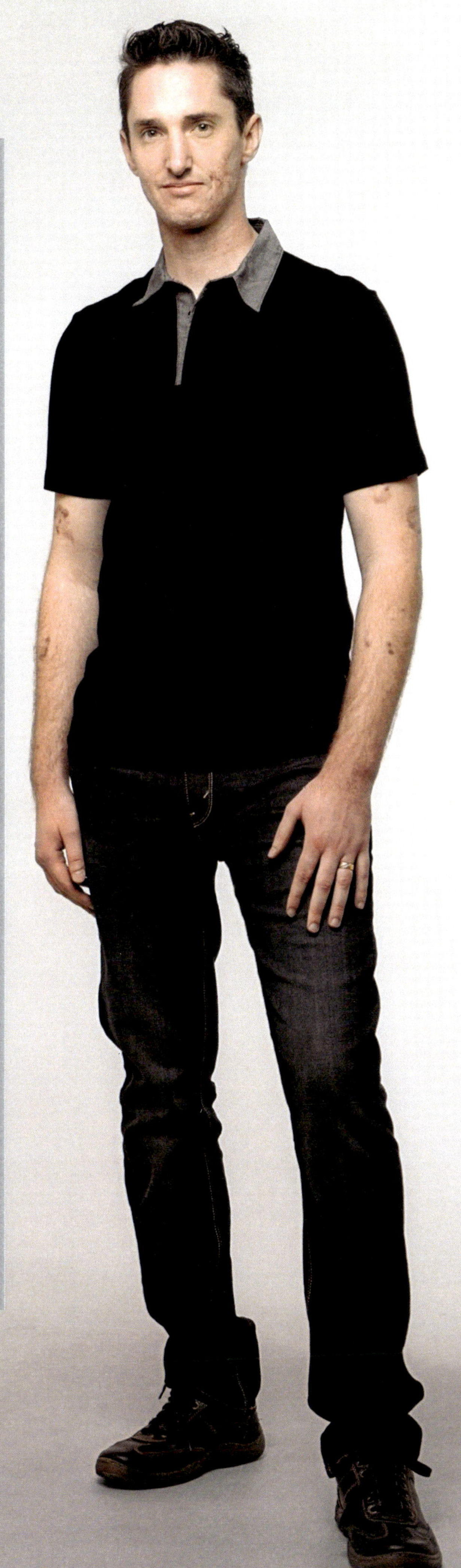

OVERVIEW

INSIDE THIS COURSE

Inside this course you will be directly exposed to the many challenges of having scars and disfigurement. You will also be introduced to methods proven to help overcome those challenges emotionally and pragmatically. If your scars or disfigurements are results of trauma or from birth then this course is for you, and whether your scars are visible or not, the lessons inside this course can be applied to your situation.

Over two decades of my own personal experience and years of collaborated research will be unfolded as common obstacles are unraveled for you to observe and learn from. Various techniques and skills will be taught that will assist you in thriving and reaching your goals.

USING THE TEXTBOOK

This course can be completed alone by a single individual, as couples or partnerships, or in group and classroom settings.

This course is also designed for your convenience. With the textbook in front of you, we are ready to begin. When you arrive at questions, take time to answer them thoroughly. An answer is not given unless it is recorded. If you're learning in a group, discuss your thoughts and responses openly and together. Ponder the questions out, but don't worry about being right or wrong. Each question is solely intended to generate ideas and help shape perspectives as we go along.

If you are unable to write or fill your answers in manually, the use of a voice recorder may be a substitute method of recording your responses.

Apply what you learn to the world in which you live. The key to progress is repetition. What doesn't start out as easy will later become natural, and then enjoyable—if you stick with it. Don't worry about what stage you are at right now in life or in the recovery process. We are all at different stages. Just think about moving forward, and you will.

It's highly recommended that you work through the course start to finish the first time. That way you know what's here and what to expect. After completion, return and concentrate on your weak areas. Focus on the parts that you want most help on as often as you feel necessary.

NOTICES AND DISCLAIMERS

The primary focus of this course is intended to alleviate the emotional effects that result from physical scars, disfigurement, and trauma, whether associated from birth or from later in one's life. This includes, but is not limited to, burns, diseases, injuries, disfiguring illnesses and birth defects. On occasion it may be found that the techniques and skills that are taught in this course may also help one overcome the invisible scars that result from mental or psychological trauma. In no way, shape, or form is this book intended to replace the advice of medical professionals at any time. Since the scope of how diverse of a population can and will be helped is uncertain, the reason for utilizing this course is entirely left to the discretion of the participant.

No claim has been made by the creator of this book or by Rare Cases LLC that the solutions to everyone's situations are going to be found in this course alone. As people are unique, so is their story. When any portion of this course serves to improve someone's life or provide him or her with added knowledge, it fulfills its designed purpose.

BACKGROUND

A LITTLE BIT OF MY STORY

My name is Brady Armstrong. The scars that I have on my face and body are from a rare case of the chickenpox virus that I had when I was six years old.

Here I am before the chickenpox.

I know it's weird, but I came very close to dying from the chickenpox. And although I survived, many scars from the experience remained, scars on the outside that everyone can see, and scars on the inside—painful, emotional scars—that have had to heal over time. After a long stay at the hospital, I immediately started down a strenuous road of physical, mental, and emotional recovery that lasted the duration of my childhood, adolescence, and well into adulthood.

You see, much like you, I never planned on having scars. I didn't want to be disfigured, and these obstacles don't simply go away. I have had to learn to accept that.

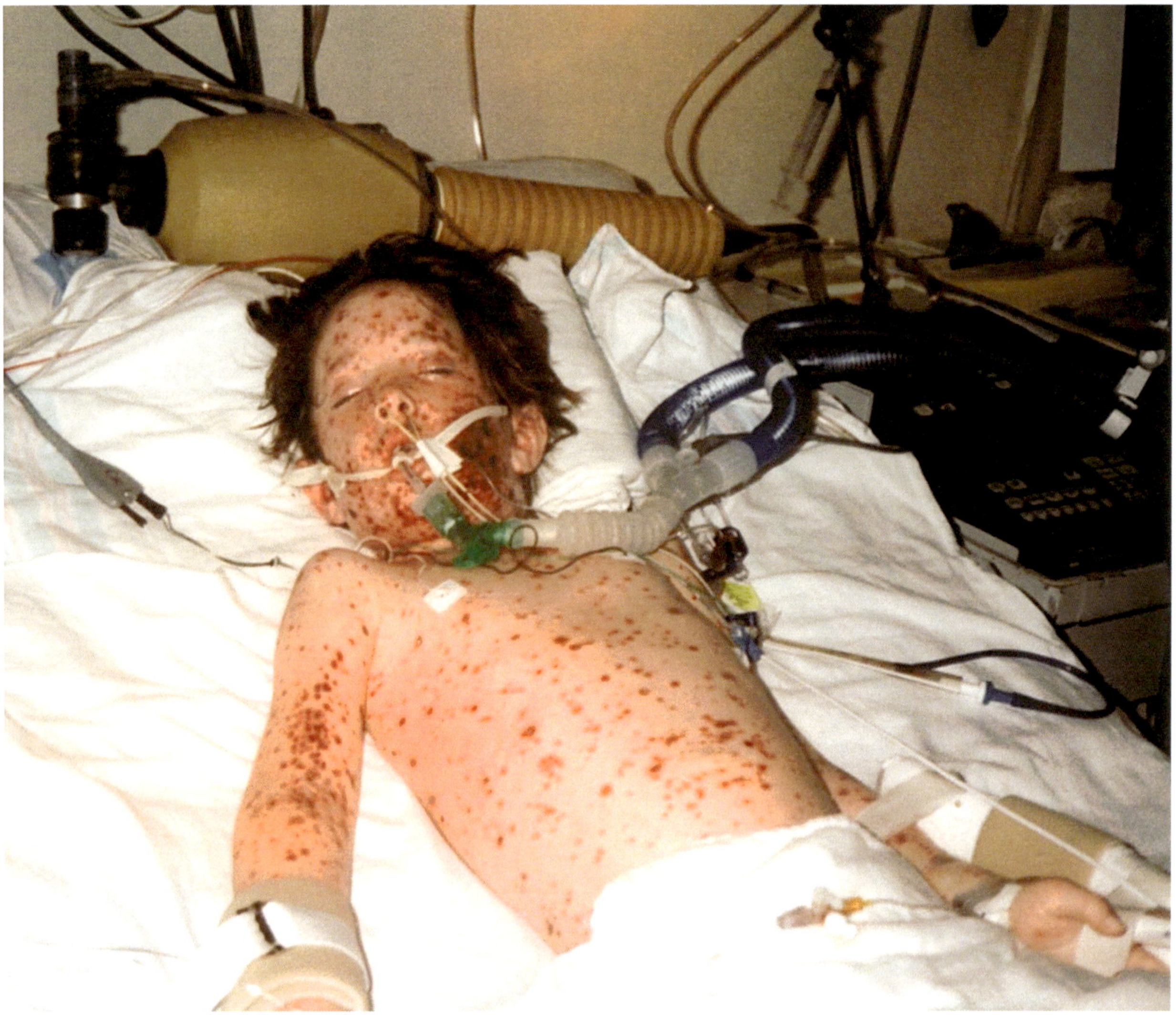

Here I am in the hospital, in a coma, my whole body covered with the disease.

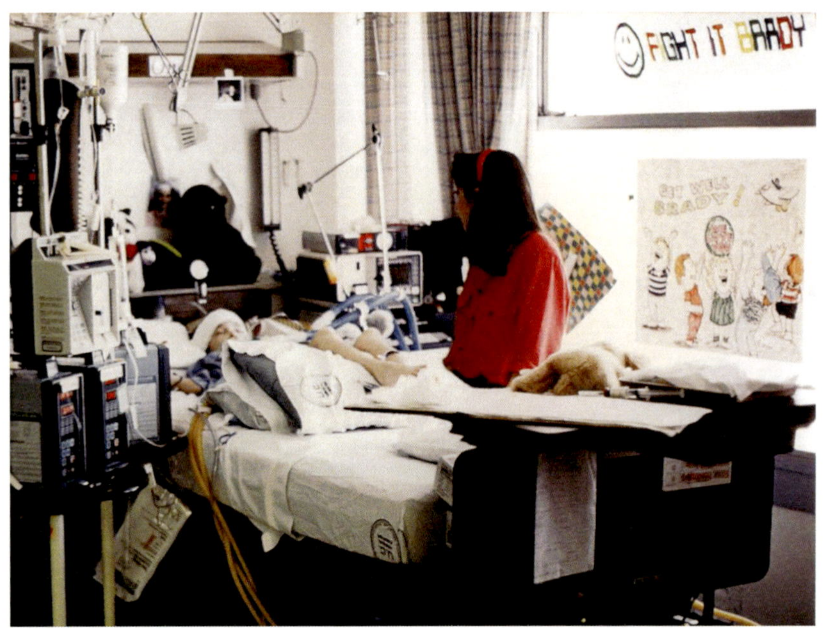

My mother and father keep constant watch over me and hope for my survival.

Here I am finally preparing to go home.

I survived the terrible illness, and thereafter I went on to attend public school from first grade through graduation, all the while attracting a lot of unwanted attention. Criticism for the way I looked was constant. Social and emotional effects continued as I went on to college, obtained various jobs, traveled the world, started a family, and launched my career.

As does anyone with scars—emotional or physical—I have had to cope, adjust, and learn to build the life I want with my scars attached. To this day, more than two decades later, the scars are still here, but they have never been in my way, or in the way of my dreams. The influence they have on my life has gone from negative to positive, but it has never diminished.

People still look. They still stare. They ask the same questions as always. Some laugh and others even make fun. Some choose to run away. These scars will be with me every single day, and these things will never cease to happen.

But some things have changed...

I no longer fear or avoid the attention of anybody. Instead, I embrace any attention I get. I appreciate the story behind my scars so much that I enjoy every opportunity to share it with other people. I would never get rid of my scars or disfigurement even if I could. I'm dead serious.

How did this change happen?

The unfortunate answer for me is TIME. Time and perseverance, but not everyone needs to suffer as much as I did, nor as long as I did. Not anymore.

Why?

Because a course like this one was never made available to me. I didn't have a mentor to walk me through the obstacles. The process of adjusting and adapting to my appearance and to society was torturous. Trial and error was the only way I knew. No one should have to go through what I did—not when there's help of the kind you will find in this textbook. I've meticulously done the laborious legwork and research for your use and benefit, so for your sake, please use it.

What inspired this course in the first place?

Occasionally, I get asked how I've managed to achieve success and enjoy so much out of life when I have to deal with these big, red, visible scars on my face every day. It's an intrusive question, but not without reason. People naturally figure that with scars and disfigurement, someone like me wouldn't generally be very ambitious or outgoing. But the truth is, many like me have a whole lot of ambition, and we succeed at our goals in spite of our disabilities and disfigurements. There shouldn't be anything, whatsoever, holding back anyone who has the desire and the determination to live a normal, successful life.

Still, many individuals struggle with their scars and with being disfigured, so I'm reaching out to the ones who do. I firmly believe that anyone can overcome the effects of scars and disfigurement, no matter the case.

For years, I've enjoyed the experience of providing guidance and insight to survivors of diverse backgrounds and being able to act as a resource to their families and friends. Understandably, survivors want help from someone who can relate to their story, and their families and friends seek help in fulfilling their role in the coping and adjustment process.

So, to continue my efforts and advocate on a broad scale to help as many people as possible, I have literally spent hundreds of hours spilling heart, sweat, and tears into developing this course.

If you are thinking something along these lines:

"Brady, your scars aren't that bad. They aren't as noticeable or as painful as mine. How can I trust that this course will benefit my situation, which is obviously much worse?"

Or,

"This course won't apply to me. No one can relate to what I'm going through, so it's not worth my time or the investment."

Then my response to you is the following:

Put it to the test. From what I've seen firsthand and by what research tells, it isn't the size, color, shape, placement, origin, or type of scar or disfigurement that makes the difference in results. The quality of your life can improve regardless of the kind of disfigurement or extremity of your scars. People with scars and disfigurement of all shapes, sizes and backgrounds are benefiting from this course, so why would you be any different?

Understand this: **Your commitment is required for this to work.** Without commitment on your end, this is just another textbook taking up space somewhere. We have to work together in order to succeed.

THE CHALLENGE

We all have scars, whether they are visible or invisible, external, or internal. Surviving any form of trauma is instinct and is only the beginning. Being able to adapt and thrive well after trauma hits is the real challenge.

Let's begin

This first section of the course allows you to get your story recorded. By answering the following questions, some of your initial thoughts and feelings will be documented. From here, you will always be able to look back and measure your progress from the very beginning. Also, by articulating these things now, you'll gain clarity and understanding of the challenges ahead.

* If you are unable to write your answers down, it is recommended that you voice record them so that you can refer back later on.

INSTRUCTIONS

The following questions lay a basic foundation and starting point for the course. Answer the questions thoroughly and to your best ability. The examples provided are one-liners, but your own answers should be elaborate and detailed.

1. Are your scars from trauma or are they from birth? How did you get them? If they're from trauma, what traumatic experiences have you survived?

Example: My scars are from a traumatic illness that I had when I was a child. I survived a rare case of chickenpox, and as result I have several scars on my face and body.

2. Describe your scars in detail. Include their type, placement, size, color, shape of the scar, etc.

Example: I have red keloid scars on my face, arms, and chest. I also have surgical scars on my chest. The most prominent scar is so large that it covers most of the left side of my face.

____

____

____

____

____

____

3. How have your scars created a negative impact on your life overall?

Example: My scars generate a lot of unwanted attention, which makes it hard to blend in with society and the general public.

____

____

____

____

4. List specific areas of life that are most influenced by your scars and how the impact on those areas has been good or bad.

Common areas of life include:
Private life – Public life – Home and family life – Social life and friendships – Life at school – Life at work/employment– Life of romance

Examples: Work and employment is influenced in a bad way because I struggle to pass job interviews. Home and family life is influenced for both good and bad because I seem to embarrass my siblings when their friends are around, but family is still my biggest line of support.

____

____

____

____

5. In your opinion, why is having your scars a bad thing?

Examples: People think I'm ugly. I don't look normal. People don't accept me for who I am.

6. Is there anything positive that has come into your life that is a result of having your scars or is a result of the trauma you experienced?

Examples: Since the trauma happened, incredible people have surrounded me. My experience has made me stronger than I was before.

7. What do you want to achieve in life that right now you feel your scars are preventing you from achieving?

Examples: I want people to find me attractive. I want to act romantic without feeling like my scars are visual barriers. I want to go to school without getting bullied because of how I look.

8. In your opinion, what needs to happen between you and your scars so that you can achieve your goals?

Examples: If I'm to achieve my goals I need to feel good about myself. People need to stop judging me poorly, or I need an operation to remove the scars permanently.

____

____

____

____

____

Sometimes the hardest part about a challenge is finding the best, most effective, and most efficient way to get started on it.

This challenge is about to get easier...

FOUR FORCES

The first step in overcoming the challenges of having physical scars or a disfigurement is recognizing what forces are against you. There are four primary forces that have endless pressure and influence on everyday living. They are:

Force 1 – The force behind one's own reactions to how they look.

Force 2 – The force behind one's own opinions on how their physical appearance affects life.

Force 3 – The force behind the reactions of other people as they react to your appearance.

Force 4 – The force behind the opinions of other people and how they compare scars to life.

Our scars and disfigurements are results and reminders of unpleasant moments in our lives. But, they are also much more than that. They are the symbols of some of life's greatest lessons. Naturally though, our own initial reactions to them can be absolute shock and repulsion. Our first opinions of them are often resentful. They represent suffering, pain, and everything that's different about us. Additionally, other people don't always react well to our appearances, and the opinions they have about us are frequently contrary to what we'd want them to be.

The forces behind reactions and opinions are so powerful that they play a large role in defining the way we live by contributing to how we conduct our behavior on a daily basis. Like four unstoppable winds, they beat down on us from all sides and cannot be avoided. Without proper sails in place, you or I can easily become caught in the turbulence of stress and despair, because as humans, we are conscientious and sensitive to what we and other people think about us. Everyone needs tools to navigate themselves through the storms of life. This section of the course titled, *Four Forces* is a sail that will help glide you along peacefully. Here, you will learn to use the strength of these forces as an aid rather than facing it as a tempest enemy. The reactions and opinions that you and other people have towards your scars or disfigurement can ultimately operate in your favor.

Just like adjusting air conditioning to the most comfortable setting, each of us can gauge the climate of our own life—we can control our reactions to meet our needs. We can be readily prepared for the reactions of other people. We can alter our opinions and influence the opinions of others to better match the atmosphere we want to live in. By learning to maneuver our way through these four forces, we can create an environment to our liking. We'll discuss each force separately; each is a milestone for achieving success on your way to adapting to your circumstances, realizing your goals, and thriving in your life.

FORCE NUMBER ONE: YOUR REACTIONS

Reactions create moods. They shape attitudes and form opinions. Our reactions are an outward display of the persona inside of us.

A couple of memories that have never left me are the two times I beheld my face in the mirror after drastic changes were made to it. The first of those times was shortly after the chickenpox virus broke out. The rash was spreading rapidly. I clearly remember standing naked in my parent's bathroom and getting ready for an oatmeal bath. The severity of the rash had become so bad, so quickly, that I no longer recognized myself in the mirror. I was terrified that I would never be the same as I was before. There really are no words to describe those emotions of knowing your body is transforming in a detestable way that is beyond your control. The second time was a few years later when a skin graph was performed. The procedure involved removing the largest scar from my face and grafting skin from behind my ears to be in its place. I was so young and innocent that I expected the procedure to deliver perfect results. When the gauze was unwrapped and the moment came for me to behold my face again, to my great disappointment, the scars, although diminished in size were still there.

To my own detriment, I had a talent for concealing my true feelings. I knew how to keep a smile and my humor alive while quietly suffering emotionally. When people asked how I was recovering, I lied and always said I was doing fine. No doubt my response was backed by a strong sense of hope, but I was also very defiant to confess to anyone how truly devastated I was. Deep down I knew I was going to be scarred for life. I was miserable, but preferred to tell a lie and say that I was fine. That deceitful reaction on my part was continually repeated for years.

Secretly, I prayed earnestly. I made a wish at every birthday and upon every star in the heavens that God would take the scars away from me. Of course, He never did. I realize that it was a silly request, but I was only a child and a magical cure like that seemed just and right at the time. It took me way too long to catch on, but finally I learned a great lesson about the way I was reacting.

The Lesson

My reactions were my problem, not the scars. My scars weren't going away. They were never going to fall off or disappear. Eventually, I came to terms with that reality. The pain and anger I was feeling wasn't from the scars at all. I was hurting on the inside, deep within my emotions, and only a change to my own reactions was going to cure that inner bitterness.

It's no surprise to me now that as I retrained myself to react more positively, the moods, attitude, and opinions I had about life and myself overall improved dramatically. Was retraining myself to react easy to do? Absolutely not. But with time, reacting differently became natural. Esteem for myself as a person incrementally grew higher, and an awareness for the bright future I was going to lead became progressively more clear.

We All React Differently

The manner in which you react to your scars by nature might be entirely inconsistent with the way I do to mine. Some people react to their scars with acceptance and grow fond of them the day they arrive. Their ability to react with a positive attitude from the start is nothing less than a gift. Most of us go through a process of coerced subjection and ongoing patience with our scars in order to gain an acceptance for them, a process of submission that, without the right help, can be long and arduous.

We're all at different stages. Our reactions are at varying degrees. No matter what stage you feel you're at right now, today you can commence to condition your reactions a little better, to a temperature that's more pleasant for you. You might have to dig real deep to find how your reactions can improve, but without question, it can be done.

The following pages contain guidelines that will help in the process of refining the way you react in a way that is organized, practical, and proficient.

GUIDELINE #1: TO CONDITIONING REACTIONS

Gauge the climate of your current life

Sara's Story

Sara was distraught, and rightfully so. She and her sons had just barely survived an accidental explosion at their home garage. How they all made it outside in time is still undetermined. All she remembers is the paramedics finding her on the front lawn and being transported to the hospital by ambulance. She would have to undergo treatment for burns on her arms, hands, and neck.

"The boys were in the garage every day last week working on a science project," she said as we sat in the dimly lit hospital room. "Why hadn't I paid closer attention to them? I'm such a horrible mother. Now we're here in the hospital for Lord knows how long. My kids are severely burned, and so am I. Our lives will never be the same. At this moment, I don't know what condition our house is in, and I have no idea where we will go if we can't go back. Brady, my life has turned completely upside down on me."

Sara and her boyfriend had broken up the month prior to the accident. Her family members resided out of state and couldn't be with her. At that point in her life, she felt absolutely alone. She was lost and overwhelmed. And as a mother, she felt the responsibility for the well-being of her two sons, but Sara did not know where to start in the recovery process. Everything in her mind was spinning. Although it only took a second for her world to blow up that winter, getting things back to normal was going to take much more time.

When I first spoke with her, Sara wanted direction. We began our discussion by filtering through the chaos and bringing things back to basics. Without building a foundation first, there was going to be nowhere for her to stand.

The same is for any of us. We all need a foundation on which to start our own recovery.

To begin building a foundation for yourself, imagine the following scenario:

Scenario:

Imagine the sensation of entering your vacant house after a long period of being away. This house of yours has been subject to adverse weather conditions and without regular maintenance. No one has stepped foot inside since your departure long ago.

Upon entering, you immediately notice how stale and hot it is. There is an odd musty smell in the air. Dust and spider webs have accumulated every-where and are even hanging from the ceiling. The clock is no longer ticking. Inquisitively, you check the electrical breakers and examine each room. As you go about, you turn on the lights and faucets to see if they still work and look for any valuable items out of place. In conclusion, you determine the house is in shambles and well overdue for some attention and repairs.

Getting your house back to the condition you want will require organization and priority setting. You need to find out what you still have and what is potentially lost. You have to decide what new things to acquire and what old things can be thrown away.

Getting your house into shape will require serious effort, but the effort is well worth it. After all, this is your home.

That short scenario described an imaginary inspection on your house. Now in a similar way, but realistically this time around, take time to inspect the condition of your current life. Observe the details of what you're experiencing. Review the events that have come and gone, both the grueling, traumatic ones as well as the rewarding ones. Notice how your body and state of mind have changed over time. Beyond the physical scars, what else is different about you? Make note of everything around you that is impacting your emotions and pushing your situation to be out of balance.

PERFORMING A LIFE INSPECTION

Like the house, your situation has been unfavorable for some time. You are scarred or otherwise disfigured, and because of that, by now things have broken. Other things are lost. Ask yourself if all of your lights are turning on. How is the plumbing? Is your body functioning the way it should? Are your spirits up? Do you have any confidence with your appearance at all? How are your relationships? Overall, are you happy? Are you headed towards the future that you want? Has trash piled up so high that you need a fresh start altogether? For some people, like in Sara's case, the house called Life has in essence burned down in its entirety. For others, only a few things need tidied up.

Think of this life inspection as introspection, where you take steps back and look within yourself to examine your current place and state. Everyone thinks about "how things are going" from time to time, but it's usually only a mental process that lasts a few minutes. This time, write down what you find so that we can use the information later on.

DOCUMENT WHAT YOU FIND

Record your life inspection so that you can prioritize needed repairs and upgrades. The following steps will help in the process:

1. **Count your blessings first and hold on to them. Don't take for granted the parts of life that are in good condition.**
2. **Record the things that need to be recovered or that can be replaced.**
3. **Make note of items that can be discarded or forgotten.**
4. **Devise a shopping list of new things to acquire as soon as possible.**

Remember, this is YOUR life inspection. Sometimes it helps to receive input and ideas from other people, but as you do, remember that no one else in this world can concisely define your happiness for you.

Space is provided below for recording what you find.

Life Inspection

1. Count your blessings first. These are things in your life that are still working and are in good condition.

Examples: I have a supportive family. The communication I have with friends is good. I have the ability to move about by myself independently.

____

____

____

____

____

____

____

____

____

2. What things in your life need to be recovered?

Examples: It's time to mend old relationships. I need to recover a physical ability, e.g. to walk, write, dance, etc. I need to get back to school. I need to get back to work.

____

____

____

____

____

____

____

3. What things in your life can be replaced?

Examples: Some bad relationships can be replaced. Some of my hobbies and talents can be exchanged for others. Houses, cars, or material goods can also be replaced.

____

____

____

____

4. What things can be discarded or forgotten?

Examples: Worthless expenses, old habits, hurtful people, etc.

____

____

____

____

5. What things do you need to acquire as soon as possible?

Examples: I need mentoring or therapy. I should get legal guidance. I need to find employment/ education.

____

____

____

____

____

____

At this point you should have completed a thorough inspection on your current life. You have taken detailed notes describing what you have found and are now ready to go onto the next step.

Continue to guideline #2

GUIDELINE #2: TO CONDITIONING REACTIONS

Adjust the thermostat and clean house

My wife and my mother would be the first ones to attest that a house out of order, if not cleaned up right away, will lead to heated reactions from them that no one wants to deal with. I confirm the accuracy in their statement.

When it comes to our own lives, most of us can relate to that. When things we care about get damaged—including our own bodies—or when people get out of line, or when things aren't going the way we'd hope, naturally, we become aggravated and disheartened.

Looking back at your life inspection, do you wish some things were different?

Living with scars or a physical disfigurement can be very troublesome, especially because you didn't choose this way of life—it was handed to you. The challenges you now face can be so great that perhaps you wish none of them were happening. The simple phrase, "I wish things were different" is a broad statement and so heavy that it slips right off the tongue. Understand that wishing things were different, that the scars weren't there, or wishing that your appearance was less peculiar or that the whole situation would change is normal. Everyone with a visible difference has had those same thoughts at some point. It might be that you're experiencing feelings of anger. Maybe you're suffering with resentment. Depression, confusion, embarrassment, shame, and an overall feeling of being lost are all honest reactions that come with the situation. When we admit to having these reactions we can begin to make positive adjustments to them. Don't hesitate in saying how you really feel, even if it hurts to do so. Don't disguise your reactions or invent false ones. If you're feeling bad about life, then darn, it's time for you to admit it! Positive change will come through honesty.

Change will instantaneously begin the very second that you put your life inspection into activation mode. This is only the first step of many, but it is a perfect place to start.

Note: Not taking action on your life inspection list is the same as walking into that vacant, disorderly house full of problems and deciding to just sit on the floor and let the problems persist. Don't expect your world to change before you change first.

When cleaning house, some people start with the easy tasks and work their way to the more aggressive ones. Others prefer to tackle the large goals first. As long as you make your way through your list, there is no right or wrong way to do it.

Like anyone, you want to feel good and happy about your situation again. When we know with a surety that we're progressing towards the goals that we ourselves have set, we're more apt to feel positive about what we're focused on. Having scars or a disfigurement doesn't prevent anyone from pursuing happiness. Only one's attitude can.

Go back and review your life inspection list again. Decide on a task that you can accomplish relatively soon. Choose something. Maybe you'll find something to replace. Maybe something will be thrown away forever. Maybe you'll acquire something you need. Whatever it is you decide to do, see that it gets done. Check it off the list, move on to the next task, and so on. Because it's your list, you can make edits, rewrite your ambitions, and even start over if needed. As you reach goals, one by one, happiness is bound to increase while stress will decrease.

From your life inspection list, what is the first goal you will accomplish?

*I will*____

____

At what date will you have this goal accomplished? Choose a realistic timeframe.

*This goal will be accomplished by*____________________.

Why did you choose this goal to be your very first accomplishment?

Examples: This is the easiest goal on my list. This is what I want to accomplish the most. This is the biggest problem I have.

____

____

____

____

How is accomplishing the items on your list going to help you long term?

Example: By accomplishing these goals, one by one, I am eliminating the current obstacles in my life and moving forward.

____

____

____

____

* By working your way through your list, you are accomplishing a series of goals that you have set for yourself. Don't stop. Work your way through your list. Keep selecting tasks and set times to have them completed.

When you feel you're ready, move on to guideline #3.

Guideline #3: To Conditioning Reactions

React with love towards the scars

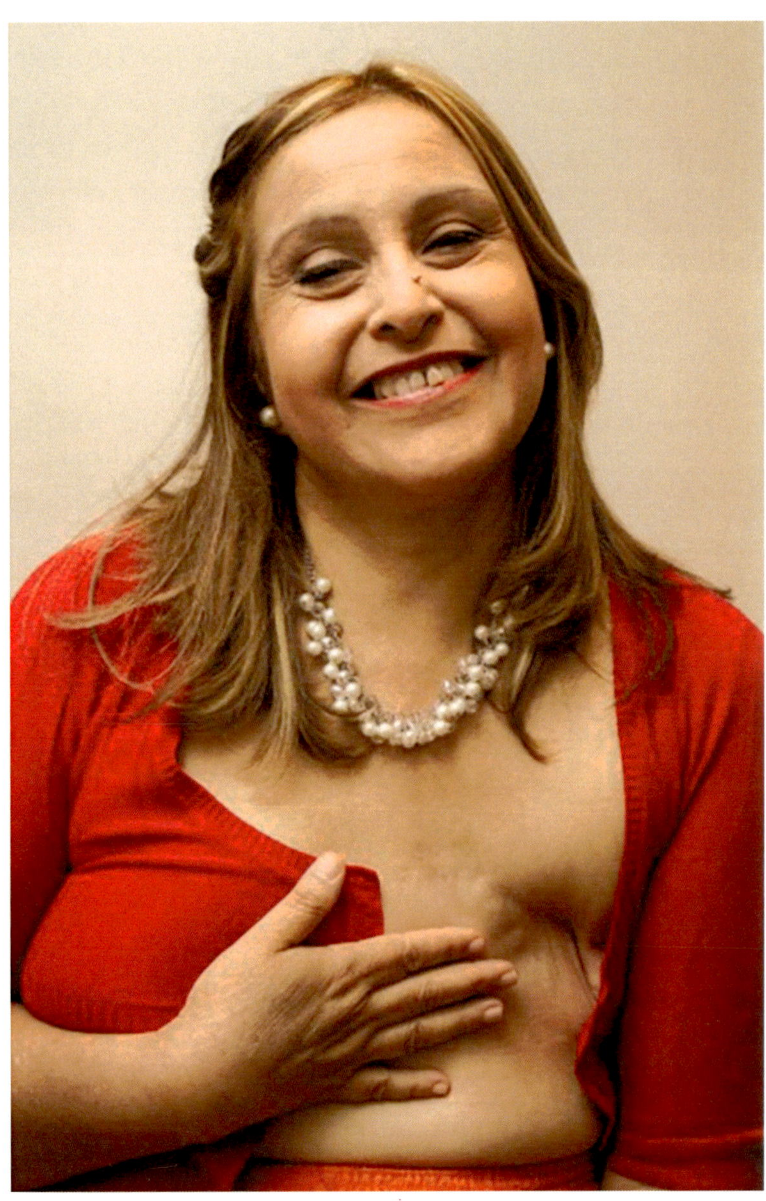

Almost unavoidably, the initial reactions that people have after being scarred permanently are shock and disbelief. Our challenges, which often seem far beyond comprehension, are signals that life is going to be drastically affected by the fact that we have an abnormal appearance. Not only do you look different, you surely don't feel the same. And if you're not physically handicapped, these changes in your appearance definitely convey that you will be impaired forever in some way.

The burdens that you will face come in many forms and they are different for each person. We're all unique. Your strengths might be my weaknesses, and vice versa. But some afflictions we share in common. Each of us, regardless of our history, is faced with emotional, psychological, personal, or social drawbacks that will have to be reckoned with eventually.

What is the correct way to react?

The correct way to react usually isn't the first reaction. The first reactions to scars are instinct. There isn't much of anything that you or I can do to control those first initial reactions. But later, with time, we can learn to react to our scars differently.

We can learn to fall in love with our story.

A passionate, sincere, heartfelt love for your own survival story is the answer. It is the correct way to react. But what about people who didn't “survive” anything to get their scars? What if you were born with yours? Whether or not you have had to “survive” trauma to get where you are today, you have survived challenges that most people won't ever get close to realizing. You're most likely taking this course because you're dealing with hurdles that the vast majority of people won't ever experience. The hurdles you face might be physical, emotional, psychological, or all of the above. These aren't minor issues. You overcome incredible odds every day, and you will continue to do so.

Take your lowest spot in life and compare it to how high you've climbed, even if it doesn't seem very far. Look back and recount the trials and triumphs you have faced thus far. That is the precise story that you need to fall madly in love with. Let me tell you why.

If you love your story then that's all that matters. If you don't love your story then everything else is going to matter. Think about this until you reach the core of what it means. If the reaction you have to your scars, disfigurement, and to the story that gave them to you is love, pure love, then no one on this planet nor any force or influence thereon can touch you! And if you don't love your story then you'll always be worried and stressed out about it.

Memorize this ridiculously catchy line with me.

“If I love my story then that's all that matters. If I don't love my story then everything else is going to matter.”

Here's proof...

Think of somebody that you loved dearly and who has died. Perhaps they're a distant relative, parent, friend, or child. Whoever they are, they were very special to you, right? Now imagine crossing someone else on the street, someone you don't know, and overhearing him or her talk horribly about this deceased loved one. This inconsiderate stranger on the street is degrading them and utterly disrespecting the legacy they have left behind. They're mocking, slandering, and carrying on belligerently. As they do this, a flood of cherished memories of you with that beloved person pour into your mind. You can't believe what you're hearing, and you're enticed to speak up and make the person stop.

At that moment, when someone talks bad about someone you love, do your feelings of love for your relative diminish or strengthen? Does the person in your heart lose or gain value?

Answer: Love for that person is strengthened and their value is increased. It's times like these when our love is reinforced. Most people would be willing to defend that kind of *love* to the grave.

Lesson: Love your own survival story in the same way. Love your scars the same way. Love your disfigurement the same way. Once we love our stories at that magnitude we become unbreakable. No matter what force we come across, if we're genuinely in love with our story, we're more than willing to defend it. We'll defend the scars, life lessons, and our life experiences to the absolute end.

Of course, not everyone is able to do this. Not everyone can fall in love with a story that has caused him or her major grief. It isn't always easy. Unfortunately, a lot of individuals wrestle with their stories their whole lives. Because of that, everything else matters to them. When insults and failed opportunities occur, it is their life story that more than likely carries the blame. That's no way to live and it's no way to treat one's self. We have to be different. It is loving the story, being grateful for it, sharing and inspiring others with it that is the best alternative reaction any of us has.

How does a genuine love for your story influence the way you react?

____

____

____

____

____

Why would some people find it difficult to love their own story?

____

____

____

____

What do you love about your story?

____

____

____

____

____

____

____

According to the above passages, when we love our stories sincerely and passionately, we're willing to defend them to the end. In what ways can someone defend a survival story?

____

____

____

____

____

____

____

Continue to guideline #4.

GUIDELINE #4: TO CONDITIONING REACTIONS

Prepare in advance to react to people

"During any given scenario, the reaction you give to other people will leave a more profound imprint on your life than the way anyone else reacts to you."

Your reactions carry more weight than anyone else's, and connected to those reactions are your mood, your attitude, and ultimately your personality. Needless to say, it's important to monitor the way you react, particularly towards other people.

Count on the fact that people are and will always be unpredictable. Some will try to hurt you, and some will befriend you. Others won't understand the trials you have to go through and will keep a distance. The value of knowing how to react to people is priceless since it is something we do everywhere we go.

The following reactions are some that we should plan ahead of time to avoid. It should be predetermined that you will refrain from reacting with these whenever prompted to:

- **Envy**
- **Shame**
- **Anger**
- **Hiding**

ENVY

A big reaction to avoid is envy. People like what they don't have more than what they have. They believe that life would be incalculably better if specific things that others enjoy were in possession by them. It's a continuous headache stemming from a combination of a human's desires, obsessions, and a belief that "the grass over there is much greener." One's perception of things can easily play tricks on the mind, and all too often it is envy that sells the illusion.

Consider the example of Clarissa, a frustrated, seventeen-year-old girl suffering with low self-esteem. Clarissa has just spent time eyeballing the photo album of a new classmate at school. To her, and based on what she sees, the classmate and her family don't have many problems. Based on what she sees in the pictures, they are always happy and having fun. They're smiling, traveling to interesting places, wearing new clothes, and living luxuriously. Life appears to be so glamorous and easy. By the time Clarissa puts the album down, she can't help but be envious.

"This girl has it all!" she thinks. "I'd be a lot happier if my life were like that."

It is her envy, however, that has Clarissa deceived. Later that hour, the new student is instructed by the teacher to introduce herself by sharing a brief history of her life to the class. The new girl talks about the pictures, her favorite memories, her hobbies, and then after a sudden pause, she changes topic. In a softer tone, she proceeds to tell the class about the many struggles that her family is currently dealing with at home.

Clarissa, sitting at the back of the room is fixed on her every word. She wasn't expecting to hear a sad story.

Beyond the colorful photographs and exciting adventures, the new girl begins to describe her twin brother, who at the start of the year was diagnosed with leukemia. “He doesn't have much longer to live,” she says. “My brother's diagnosis was a shock to everyone. Normally, I wouldn't talk about it, but I want to share this difficult part of my life. You see, my brother means the world to me, and my story wouldn't be complete without him.”

Clarissa is stunned. This girl's situation is much different from what she had previously imagined. The picture album represents only a very small fraction of the girl's life. The pictures she envied have new meaning. The glamorous life that she thought she saw was actually too few of the golden memories this family would probably ever have together. Indeed, they were facing very severe challenges—challenges which Clarissa wouldn't even consider bartering for her own. There's no denying that things are not what they had seemed.

The message in this narrative can be applied to a myriad of situations that all of us encounter.

Things aren't always what they seem.

Just like Clarissa, we cannot judge or measure someone else's quality of life when we only see small pieces of it. Of course, this lesson goes both ways. No one should judge you or I on a whim, but let's focus for a moment on our side of the table.

If you ever find yourself in the mode of saying, “If only I were them” or “If only I had what that person has” then understand that your envy might be deceiving you. If you were really grateful for your story and were living up to your potential, as a survivor should be, you'd see that most people are not so much better off than you.

I bring this up because envy is not something miniscule in the community of the scarred and disfigured. There are many reasons why one of us could envy the lifestyle of individuals who don't have a visible difference. One common reason for envy is the fact that physical appearance plays a major part in many facets of societal living, and at first glance people without scars and disfigurement have an abundance of advantages over us. Considerable categories of life including romance, school, the workplace, and public roles have an unfair trend, since people will often discriminate against physically abnormal appearances. Individuals without scars customarily don't have to try as hard in certain basic tasks like impressing a mate, making friends, or passing job interviews, and because of this polarized effect, envy is a strong reaction among our population. Many have the presumption that the road leading to success is predominantly in favor of people without visible differences, and consequentially, people of our community are often left caged with disappointment.

HOW TO AVOID REACTING WITH ENVY

Compare yourself to who and where you aspire to be in life instead of comparing to other people.

Try thinking for a minute like a strong athlete does. An athlete knows that world records are never beat simply by winning races. If everyone in a race is slow, being the fastest slow person is not impressive. Ask any professional track and field athlete if their true race is against fellow runners or against the clock. They will tell you that a runner becomes fast only by racing against time. Wanting the stamina and strength of another runner does not increase their speed. Studying the abilities and techniques of fellow athletes can help, but only fewer seconds on the stopwatch makes the difference in the end.

We're not talking about being in or winning a race, but in order to rid ourselves of envy, we have to think identically to how an athlete does. We have to compare ourselves to our own progress without dwelling on the condition or the progress of others.

Replace sayings like "I wish I was like them" and "If only I had what they have" with self-motivated thoughts and intuitions such as "I will do whatever it takes to be able to __________;" "I will have __________;" and I will be more __________." These may seem like small adjustments to the way we speak and think, but the discrepancies between them are far reaching. Don't underestimate the force behind words and thoughts. Sometimes all we need to change is our language.

How was envy deceiving in Clarissa's example?

____

____

Why is envy a common reaction among people with scars and disfigurement?

____

____

____

In what way should we think similar to how an athlete thinks?

____

____

SHAME

If it hasn't happened to you already, people will come along with some very creative insults. Hecklers and bullies are like bacteria; more of them are born while others finally die off or turn into something productive—like in yogurt and cheese.

There are two rules of thumb when it comes to bullies and insults.

1. Don't plan on bullies ever going away because they won't.

2. Don't take insults personally.

A mistake that many commit is the act of getting offended by something that's either said or done to them. Getting offended is the direct result of letting your emotional guard down. Such an act should never take place. Feeling shame is even worse than getting offended, and lamentably, it is another reaction regularly experienced by individuals with scars and disfigurements.

Shame has both profound meaning and grim consequence. It is a painful feeling resembling disgrace, and the consequence of reacting with shame is that when we do, we surrender our love for the story and replace love with regret.

Can you love your story and feel shame for it at the same time?

Answer: You cannot.

When someone insults you and you feel shame, it's the same as believing every word the person says and telling yourself that you deserve it. It's basically like them handing you a goblet of poison that you willingly drink. Reversely, if someone insults you and you love your story, unconditionally, then any poisonous words projecting from their lips disintegrate in mid-air, leaving you undamaged and untouched. So remember, when it comes to your scars, disfigurements, trials, achievements, and life story, by reacting with shame you do the opposite of what you should, which is to react with love.

When we feel shame for our story, the love we have for it is replaced with what?

____

____

How is reacting with shame like drinking poison?

____

____

Explain how reacting with shame is the opposite of reacting with love?

____

____

ANGER

What you know to be true is more powerful than anything that anyone can say or do to you. Because you have this knowledge, there is no reason to get angry.

Avoid getting angry. This rule is as straightforward and self-explanatory as it sounds. Any temperament that would lead you to retaliate against an offender should be avoided. There are people out there who will go to great lengths to make your appearance into a public freak show—a phenomenon—just because they don't like the way you look. Yes, it is a careless, gutless, and ignorant way to demonstrate their opinions, but they will do it, and regardless of what they do, for your own sake, never react with anger or revenge.

A reaction of anger, hatred, or any degree of retaliation towards an offender will only make the situation worse for you long term. Undoubtedly, the demeanor by which you react to others will always leave a more profound imprint on your life than the way anyone else reacts to you. By reacting to insults and mockery with anger, you slowly and surely become short tempered, impatient, and quick to seek retribution. These are attributes that no one should want on a life resume.

Where justice is rightfully deserved, justice can also be served to an offender by calmly utilizing the correct resources and without exerting anger.

How does reacting with anger make things worse for you over time?

____

____

____

____

____

HIDING

You might be able to hide your scars, but you cannot hide from them. There are very distinct differences between the two.

Hidden Scars

Public places can be congruent to a circus where you feel that you are a spectacle in a sideshow. Because of that, sometimes we believe it's best to escape the way the public makes us feel through hiding. Hidden scars are scars that can be covered up and kept out of sight. A mother's stretch marks from giving birth, or injuries to the chest, back, and thigh are prime examples of hidden scars. Hidden scars can also include the emotional traumas that we feel but refuse to reveal. One has the ability to keep a hidden scar out the public eye forever. Yet, out of sight out of mind is only temporary relief. Remove the shield, expose the scar, and the embarrassment they feel will often return full-fledged.

For optimum advice, don't become unhinged by overexerting yourself to avoid embarrassment by keeping your scars hidden. A slippery slope to paranoia begins at the brink of when we believe we have to either conceal our scars or hide from them.

Take my own past as an illustration. My most prominent scar is on the left side of my face. During childhood I formed a really bad habit of keeping people drawn as much to my right side as possible. In a way, I was hiding. If people wouldn't see my scars as much they also wouldn't concentrate on them. At least I thought so. As you can imagine, keeping people drawn to the right side of my face was a tedious exercise and completely unnecessary. To pull it off, I was literally doing circles everywhere I went. At the grocery store or mall, for example, I would hide behind cereal boxes or hats to cover my left profile as best I could. I'd strategically stand behind my parents while we waited in lines or when standing in a crowd, using their larger frames as a protective wall for me to shroud behind. If I was at a movie theatre, on bleachers at a ball game, or at a lunch table, I would sit with my elbow upright with the palm of my hand covertly resting on the left side of my face so that no one would see my scar, or ask me questions, or get lost in an obtrusive stare. I sat down, stood up, and walked on the left side of people, to keep them as far away from the scar as I could. And I did these things with a conviction that somehow I was making the situation more pleasant. The honest truth is that I wasn't doing anything productive at all.

The routine of hiding is utterly pointless and is a total waste of time. When I thought I was making things better, the tasks involved only made me feel worse. Looking back now I can see I was downright paranoid! Think of all of the time and energy spent for nothing. I was so wrapped up in other people's reactions when I was the one reacting foolishly. Too much of my life was spent wandering around erratically like that.

Please learn from my mistakes. You can't hide from your scars, so don't even try. The way to overcome embarrassment isn't by avoiding it; the way is through building immunity by exposing yourself to it.

Keep your clothes on. No one is saying you need to go about exposing your hidden scars to the world in order to overcome embarrassment. But if and when your scars are detected, observed, criticized, examined, or questioned by other people, the best thing to do is embrace the moment as an opportunity to share.

What does the saying "You can hide your scars, but you cannot hide from them" mean to you?

____

____

Have you ever tried to hide from your scars? Have you ever achieved anything by hiding? Why or why not?

____

____

SHARING

The most underappreciated human attribute is curiosity, and you and I have the opportunity to feed curiosity often with words of experience.

Questions contain a power that is reciprocal for the asker and the answerer. As knowledge grows within anyone, the soul is edified and enriched while mental stature is matured. People want to learn from the moment they are born. You and I are no different. We are all curious people. You and I are in a very treasured position though. We are capable of providing people with a unique brand of knowledge through our stories.

Don't fear questions directed at your scars, disfigurement, or to the story that gave them to you. Those questions will never stop coming as long as you live. A fear of curiosity will surely bring you endless torment. Of course the opposite is equally true. If you appreciate curiosity in people and delight in your ability to answer questions, then you will enjoy endless pleasure in doing so.

Share Your Story

Most likely, not a lot of time will pass before the next opportunity arises where you can share your story with someone. The occasion is bound to come soon, and whenever it happens to be, share your story with a little more detail than you have in past conversations.

The sharing experience can be enjoyable and stress free when our responses are prepared in advance. I recommend having three versions on hand that vary in length of which you can select to use, depending on how much time you have to share.

Your story doesn't have to be memorized verbatim, but you'll be better off if you can spontaneously recite a summarized version of what happened to you at any given time.

The best sharing experiences come when we tell our stories like a storyteller would, without feeling overly nervous or caught off guard when compelled to do so.

Activity

Directions: Use the scenarios provided to practice telling your story. For a short response you are answering someone's question in one or two sentences only. A medium response contains a good handful of sentences describing what happened to you, and a large response gives your full detailed account. Examples are provided.

A Short Response: Imagine you are standing on a public bus and the next drop off location is yours. One block away from your exit, the teenager behind you taps you on the shoulder and asks what your scars are from. What is the response you give before the bus comes to a halt?

Example: When I was a child I had a really bad case of the chickenpox virus that left me with many scars on my face, arms, and body. I'm fine now though. Thank you for asking.

What is your short response to the teenager?

____

____

____

A Medium Length Response: You've now changed to another bus and are traveling to a nearby town. A middle-aged man takes the seat next to yours and politely introduces himself as Brian. He is quiet most of the ride, but you notice him glancing your way periodically. Five minutes before he gathers his bags together to leave, Brian tells you that his nephew was recently burned in a fire and he is curious how your scars came about. What is your response to Brian?

Example: Thank you for asking, Brian. I wasn't burned, but my scars often give the impression that I was. When I was six years old, I endured a severely rare case of the chickenpox virus that erupted all over my body. I nearly died from the illness, and these scars are what are left over.

What is your medium response to Brian before he leaves?

____

____

____

____

____

____

A Long Response: Brian gets off the bus. Right away the woman seated behind you comes and takes the seat to your side. She is very energetic, kind, and probably in her early thirties. She introduces herself as Laura and says she couldn't help but overhear your conversation with the man who had just left. Laura is intrigued by what she heard so far and wants to learn more. She remains with you until you both depart the bus at the next town. Knowing you'll have more time to talk, you decide to give her a full detailed account. What is your response?

Example: I'm glad you have found interest in my story. Like I told the man who recently left, my scars are from a severely rare case of the chickenpox virus that I had when I was young. The virus erupted all over my body, and I nearly died from it. The blisters from the chickenpox were not only on the outside of my skin, but on the inside of my body also. They were in my mouth, down my throat, and even inside my lungs.

Because of how severe of a case I had, I was hospitalized, placed on a respirator, and in a coma for a long period of time. Eventually, I had to learn to eat and walk all over again. The good news is that I survived and am here today.

The scars you see are what are left from that important part of my life. They are not only reminders of what happened at that particular time when I was young; they also represent many more experiences that have happened since then.

Having these scars has helped me understand the best ways for me to communicate with people. They have taught me to have perseverance and confidence in myself. Because of the lessons I've learned along the way, I have been able overcome many obstacles. I might look different, but I feel great!

What is your long response to Laura?

By having three different versions of your story planned and on trigger mode you are prepared to respond to almost anyone. Again, don't feel like you need to memorize these responses word for word. Once you become familiarized and fluent with sharing the details of your story, sharing becomes easier. When you are comfortable with talking about your experiences and you don't escape opportunities to share them, you have fulfilled the purpose of this exercise.

Rehearse

It can be difficult to articulate the swirl of thoughts and feelings that are wrapped up in a dramatic story. All of us want to capture the swirl of thoughts and feelings we have. Marrying the experience with words that not only fit, but also harmonize with our emotions can be hard. That's why it is crucial that we take the time to plan our responses ahead of time.

Practice by rehearsing your story alone. Start by describing what makes you different and talk out loud about the events you have been through. Expound on the lessons you've learned and how your life has been impacted so far. It's okay to start slow. Repeat and practice rehearsing often. As you become more expressive to yourself, you'll be more capable of sharing the same things aloud with other people.

Not everyone is born to be an extrovert or a public speaker, and thank goodness for that! The message isn't to push you to be more outgoing; it is simply about gaining confidence, dignity, and self-respect. Anyone can appreciate their story if they learn to openly share it with others.

End of Force #1. Continue to Force #2.

FORCE NUMBER TWO: YOUR OPINIONS

On a scale of differing opinions, your own opinion will always outweigh anyone else's. Whether you agree or disagree with me on that... well... that's your opinion.

Have you ever had the opinion that your scars or disfigurement are blocking your path and impeding you from accessing your dreams? Have you ever told yourself that you will never be able to do something that you really want to do just because you have a visible difference? If not, if you never have, count yourself among the exclusive. Opinions like these are very prevalent and natural to have given the situation.

Our opinions affect our actions and overall behavior. For this, they should always promote our own progress and well-being. Your outlook on life is a reflection of your character, and your opinions about yourself directly produce actions that echo your thoughts and beliefs.

Question: Are you capable of altering your opinions?

A. I don't know.

B. I am if you say so.

C. No, I'm too stubborn.

D. Yes, definitely!

If we are able to change our opinions about politics, religion, or our favorite color, then why not about the way we feel about ourselves? Any one of us most definitely can alter our opinions.

Lessons 2B Learned

If adhered to, these fundamental lessons will help in producing some of the best opinions that you can have about yourself and about the world you live in.

LESSON #1: Opinions don't = truth.

The following phrases are opinions that are frequently repeated by individuals with scars or a disfigurement. Perhaps you have had similar thoughts to some of them from time to time.

"Nobody wants to be close to me."

"I will never fall in love simply because of how I look."

"I will never be kissed. No one wants to kiss someone looking like me."

"I can't get a job. It's impossible to pass an interview looking like this."

"Popular and famous people don't have scars like mine."

"I can't make genuine friends. My friends will always feel sorry for me."

"All the kids at school think I look like a freak."

"There is no way I could ever appear in public like this."

"I will always be bullied."

"I can't help but look terrible in photographs."

"I can't accept what has happened to me."

And the list goes on.

What opinions have you had, believing that something can't happen, won't happen, or is not possible?

____

____

____

____

____

____

____

____

These statements are all one-sided, biased opinions. Most are based on feelings of remorse or hopelessness. These phrases and more like them are repeated all the time. It is actually very easy to fall into this pattern of speech because it's common to believe that people with visible differences are automatically subject to a life of lower quality than people without. But that simply isn't true. Unfortunately, opinions like these often carry adverse side effects. They can certainly lead to depression, and chances are they will also convert into reality due to a lack of motivation.

Don't allow yourself to be overwhelmingly convinced that the obstacles ahead of you cannot be overcome. We can change our opinions and create the opposite effect—results in our favor!

Some things that you will *never* know are what's going to happen, what everyone thinks, and what people will end up doing; so don't live on assumptions. If you shut the door in front of you with blind opinions, then advancing with an open mind is impossible. Instead, let's shut the door of ignorance behind us!

The following opinions sound a lot better...

"People find me unique and intriguing. People want to be close to me."

"I will find true love because someone will love how I look."

"I will have my first kiss and then many kisses will follow after that!"

"I will pass this next job interview."

"There are many interesting and successful people that have scars just like me."

"I can make genuine friendships. My friends care deeply about me."

"All the kids at school think I'm awesome."

"I go into the public all the time. Public places don't faze me at all."

"Bullies will be bullies, but nothing they do offends me."

"I'm very photogenic; plus, I'm easily recognized."

"I appreciate the things that have happened to me."

Keep this list going. Write down five positive opinions to your favor, specifically about yourself and the things you aim to achieve.

1.____

2.____

3.____

4.____

5.____

LESSON #2: Be your own best friend.

Friends are extremely important. I can honestly say I have many friends, but only a few do I consider to be the best of friends. My wife is by far my best friend. I have three other friends whom I consider best friends outside of family—and then there is me. I am also my own best friend. You can tell a best friend when they stand by you no matter what. They don't betray you. Ever. They proactively watch out for you. A best friend is also your strongest motivator and is gifted with perpetual encouragement.

It's easy to be our own critic and dwell on the things we're lacking as well as the things we wish we didn't have. Ceaseless criticism and nagging will undeniably take you into a never-ending cycle headed nowhere. Stop spinning around and around. Adopt a more friendly approach to life and go places.

Create the opinion that YOU are your own best friend. Say it, and then be it. Always be true to that commitment in every thought, word, and deed. Remember, as a true friend you don't beat yourself up. Build yourself up. This simple, elementary lesson is one of the most scholarly life changers of all.

What can you can do to improve your friendship with yourself? Name five.

1.____

2.____

3.____

4.____

5.____

LESSON #3: Forgive

Forgiveness is a process that makes pain disappear, but it is also a process that cannot be rushed. Moving on and developing your life to the potential it can be is going to be nearly impossible without mustering the ability to forgive an offender. Most of us have more scars on the inside emotionally than on the outside physically, and they are the scars that are carved into us the deepest. When the heart is beaten or broken apart, and our emotions are tattered with injustice, love and hope become foreign.

Enmity, animosity, and distrust are brick walls that surround us when we don't forgive. We alone create the dams that limit us, and we'll continue to do so until we decide to tear them down. If anything in your past has you so hell-bent that you cannot forgive, then right now you are pinned to the floor, immovable. Face this fact: You aren't going anywhere freely until you let go of whatever it is that has you tied down. Only when you release the bounds of condemnation for your trespassers will you move onward.

Let go of whatever it is. Forgiveness doesn't mean surrendering, nor does it offer anyone or anything defeat over you. To the contrary, forgiving means victory for you because by forgiving, you release the powers against you. Only when you forgive are you truly free.

Think of the person or event that has hurt you the most. When the time comes and you can honestly say, "I forgive you" to them, you will have claimed victory. You will have positioned yourself to never get hurt by them again. And, at that time, what used to be a burden will no longer be.

Directions: When the time is right, only you can say it is right. Fill in the blanks.

Dear ____, *I forgive you.*

Sincerely, ____

LESSON #4: Understand your limits and then defy them.

Your potential is without limit. Form the opinion that you are capable of achieving great things. Choose the milestones that you want to accomplish in your lifetime. Scars are a part of you; they accompany you everywhere you go, but they are not blocking your way. Scars can actually catapult you forward in the direction you want to go if you allow them to.

The milestones that you might have believed were unreachable you can actually reach, and the events that you might have thought will never happen just may.

Write down three *new* milestones to complete during your lifetime. These are three future achievements that you need to take seriously. Make an oath to yourself that you will check them off when completed.

1.____

____

2.____

____

3.____

____

Find someone to share your list of milestones with. Tell somebody what you are going to do, even if you know they'll think you're crazy. By talking about what our ambitions are they become more of a reality. Next, go and do them!

* You are now officially accountable for accomplishing these milestones.

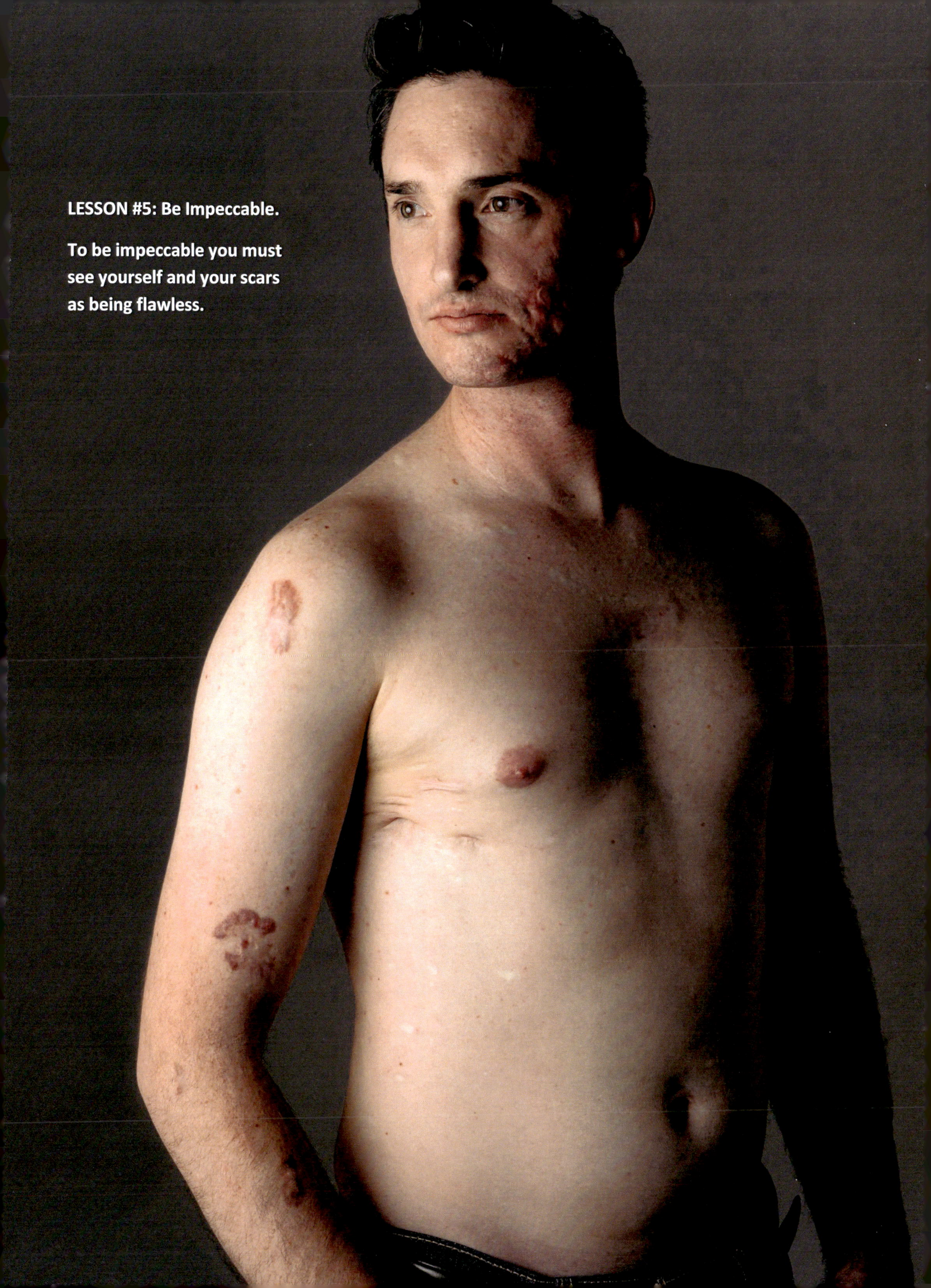

LESSON #5: Be Impeccable.

To be impeccable you must see yourself and your scars as being flawless.

I know you're not perfect, and nor is anyone, but realize that any negative opinions you have about your scars or disfigurement aren't doing you any good.

Give up the opinion that your scars are also flaws. They aren't. Replace that opinion with the belief that your scars make you complete. They are composed of a priceless story—your story. Scars testify of power, strength, knowledge, and wisdom. They are emblems of your past and are tokens of your experience. Don't belittle them.

Your life would not be complete without your scars, and you would neither be as extraordinary or as interesting without them. Thanks to having scars you are unique, singular, and different.

You should think about your scars favorably. Be grateful for all that they stand for and for what they represent. Think about the lessons you've learned by having them and about how you've grown through trial and experience. Think of the things you've lived through. When you are able to think about these things positively, constantly, you'll reach a standard of living that is free of remorse and self-pity.

Be impeccable. You have one life in this body. If this life is to be a life with scars, then make the most of it. Don't live in emotional pain. Don't count yourself as a victim of bad luck or of bad fortune. You are none of those things. Your body has changed; now change your mindset. Be impeccable.

How do your scars testify of your power, strength, knowledge, and wisdom?

____

____

____

____

____

____

LESSON #6: The world is not against you.

Believe it or not, the world wants to see you succeed. Of course there are people out there who would delight in seeing you as an easy target for failure, but there is no need to give them any attention.

The grand majority of people love a success story. By seeing you rise to an incredible height from what would appear to be rock bottom, people are blown away with astonishment. When success happens, it's exciting and inspiring. I'm sure you know how it is. Read the story of someone overcoming serious odds, and you'll have feelings of aspiration, inspiration, and ambition to do the same.

Your story of overcoming adversity, pain, and humiliation is nothing less than a success story. You must see it that way. So many people are waiting to be inspired by you. Impressing others is not the end goal, but acquiring fulfillment is everyone's end goal. Encouragement is a powerful force that you'll receive from many, so allow the encouragement you receive to propel you forward.

Break out of your shell and strive to accomplish the things that you thought were impossible. As you do, the world will cheer you on.

Project: Take your story to the next level. What can you do to share your story, your *Life with Scars* on a broader scale? How can you use your story to inspire others?

What can you do to guarantee that your story doesn't become forgotten over time?

Everyone can do something more with their story. Some have chosen to write a book, give a speech, volunteer at burn support groups, cancer groups, or participate in fundraisers for injured veterans. There is an endless list of options available to you and creativity has no limit. It's time to think outside the box. Get outside of your box. Even if you choose to do something small, doing something more is better than not doing anything else. Take your story to the next level, whatever level that happens to be.

Directions: Answer the questions and plan a project that details how you will take your story to the next level.

How do you plan to take your story to the next level? What specifically do you plan to do?

Example: I will create an inspirational video that tells my story.

____

____

____

____

____

____

____

____

How will the completion of this project increase the value of your story?

Example: This video will be broadcast on the Internet so that people everywhere can learn from it.

___

___

___

What resources do you need to achieve completion of these goals?

Example: Camera, set, props, script, music, editing software, computer to start.

___

___

___

How will you begin your project? List the first steps you will take. Include the date, time, and place where these things will happen.

Example: Starting Friday June 12th the script will begin. After the script, I will start to accumulate pictures.

___

___

___

___

How will you measure your progress?

Example: Progress will be measured by the completion of the video and the amount of views it receives.

___

___

___

___

Record your progress here.

Example: Script is complete July 1st; supplies are purchased and video is under production.

Upon successful completion, describe what you have achieved.

Example: Video is posted online and has received 100+ views! It is exciting to see this kind of response.

End of force #2.

FORCE NUMBER THREE: THEIR REACTIONS

Some things are not controllable. How other people react is one of them. Don't fret over things you cannot control, but always be ready for them.

Isn't it gratifying when someone greets you for the first time, and they don't show the slightest sign of suspicion for what happened to you to create the scars? If you're like me, this doesn't happen often. I've got a knack for recognizing curiosity in most people, especially when it's geared towards me, and I've found that most people are curious to know what happened.

It's imperative to realize that we are incapable of preventing offensive reactions altogether. We'll witness reactions of every kind from people. Some will be spontaneous while others will be planned out. Controlling how people will react to us is impossible. The most we can do is be ready for them.

We're about to explore a list of common reactions that other people can have when shown your scars for the first time. Usually it's a combination of reactions happening simultaneously. Reactions can be subtle, but can also be outwardly intrusive. Depending on the setting and environment, each reaction is capable of producing some degree of distress if you are not adequately prepared for it. To be fully equipped in training, you'll want solid awareness as to what reactions to expect.

We'll take a detailed look at the following common reactions:

- **Politeness**
- **Staring**
- **Pointing**
- **Curiosity**
- **Indirect approaches**
- **Sorrow**
- **Withdraw**
- **Embarrassment**
- **Fear**
- **Disgust**
- **Ridicule**

POLITENESS

When someone is polite, you'll notice that they're intentionally avoiding the placement of their energy and attention focused on your scars. They will direct eye movement and verbal interaction to other areas in effort to conceal their curiosity, but you sense them periodically catching a quick glance at you when you're not looking.

What do you do when you find this kind of politeness in people?

____

____

____

____

____

Useful Tips: Allow the person to be polite. There shouldn't be an urgency to satisfy their curiosity immediately. Answers can be given to them over time if the relationship carries on. For brief encounters, find humor in their discreet behavior. Don't find reasons to be offended when a person is only trying to be polite. If effective communication requires all uneasiness to cease, bring the topic of your scars to the table by exhibiting an even greater amount of politeness.

Notes

____

____

____

____

STARING

You get the feeling that you are being heavily examined. Quite frankly, you are. People naturally seek comfort in their surroundings, and inspecting something they find to be abnormal (even a strange face or someone's appearance) is totally normal behavior. Some will stare at you point blank, but most will stare with the mistaken belief that they are under your radar. Your sixth sense knows better. You can sense a stare a mile away.

What do you do when you know someone is staring at you?

____

____

____

____

____

Useful Tips: Understand why people stare, and don't get offended by it. Allow everyone the chance to feel comfortable with you around. This means allowing them time to look. Interrupting a stare is counterproductive, for the sooner the observer gathers the information they need for their own comfort, the sooner your interaction will either proceed to the next level or cease altogether.

A stare has some resemblance to a computer screen that is downloading data or a program. Once the information has transmitted completely, the waiting game is over and interaction can begin.

At times you might find people who simply won't stop staring. Curiosity has them confounded. At this point you might find it constructive to either offer them a closer look through conversation, or leave altogether. Some find it better to friendly approach the person rather than shun them when they're trying to process information. Offering a closer look is an action that demonstrates confidence on your part and attentiveness to their interest in you.

Notes

____

____

____

____

____

POINTING

Public scrutiny begins to escalate when someone has the nerve to single you out with a gesture that draws additional attention in your direction. Pointing is an action usually founded on an effort to attract numerous views and remarks from multiple sources. At this moment you become a target object of review, a situation that can become severely uncomfortable as you may feel degraded and publicly demeaned.

What things have you noticed happening when people are pointing at you and how have you chosen to handle the situation?

____

____

____

____

Useful Tips: Increase your cognitive awareness to what is happening overall, and decrease your emotional connection to what is being said and heard. You know what's happening, but it doesn't need to offend you. No response on your part is required, but if you feel that you must respond to the gestures and control the incoming traffic of surveillance, be bold enough to say something that does not entice mockery, and do it in a way that demonstrates a serene and solid composure. My simple response is usually a cordial, "Thank you for noticing me. Is there a question I can answer for you?"

Understand, someone who is going to point at you out of spite is not concerned about anyone but themselves. The meaning of the gesture changes dramatically when they point from astonishment and shock, or when they point with hostility.

Remember, the purpose of pointing is to draw attention to you. You will undoubtedly have everyone's attention, so use this moment as an opportunity to demonstrate that you are not only unique, but also balanced and poised with self-confidence.

Notes

____

____

____

____

CURIOSITY

Everyone is curious, but now curiosity has carried someone far enough that they ask a question—a direct question, too. "What happened to you?" or "Why do you look that way?" They will ask these questions in private settings and they will ask where others can hear and listen in as well. Sometimes they will be loud and rude about it. Decide now what your reply will be.

What direct questions have you already been asked and how have you answered them?

____

____

____

____

Useful Tips: A requisite for thriving in a world populated with curious human beings is to gain a genuine appreciation for questions. Curious people will bring you either torment or alleviation. You decide what it will be.

Become a storyteller. Not everyone has a gift for telling a captivating story, but storytelling is incontestably a talent you can acquire over time. People inherently enjoy stories, and you will see that when people become engaged in yours, a sincere affection for you as the survivor, the champion of the story, will grow within your audience.

If you choose to evade questions about your scars, it will be interpreted that you're ashamed of them. Many people already have a prior inclination that you are ashamed. It pains them to imagine what it's like to have scars like yours. When you don't talk openly about it, you reinforce the inclination that you're suffering. The result is people feeling sorry for you. You don't want pity, you want commendation, so don't be afraid to be zealous. Celebrate your life by answering questions and by sharing your story.

Notes

____

____

____

____

INDIRECT APPROACHES

Somehow you find out that a relative or close friend was approached by a third party and was asked about your scars. This is very common. People have the notion that their questions will offend you, but they can't resist curiosity and want answers. For them, it's less intrusive to go the indirect approach and ask someone else with whom they can confide.

Realize that your relative or friend in this situation may or may not be ready to share your story for you. They might not feel comfortable talking about it. Maybe they don't want you to find that they were sharing your information behind your back. Perhaps they are perfectly fine with giving the answer, but either you or they feel that their answer is not adequately prepared. It would be great if relatives and friends were always ready to give the correct response, but often that's not the case.

How do your friends and family respond in your behalf when an indirect approach comes their way?

____

____

____

____

Useful Tips: Training everyone close to you to respond to indirect approaches individually is not a feasible proposition. Don't stress about contacting everyone you know on the topic; nonetheless, the significance of what you are communicating to family and friends is exactly where you should focus your attention.

Family and friends—the people closest to you—need to have sound understanding that you are not a victim to your scars. Their perception of your situation should mirror how you feel, but getting them to that point might take a reasonable amount of time. Loved ones carry a deep sense of sorrow for the predicament that you have been forced to live with, so for them recovering from that sorrow is a healing process of its own. Many loved ones will claim part ownership of your scars out of love and with a desire to help carry the burden. You can assist them by demonstrating that there is no burden left to carry.

When friends and family are able to grasp the message that you have grown fond of your scars and actually love your story, they become apt to follow in your footsteps. Reinforce this conviction through the senses. Let them see it in your behavior. Let them hear it in your words, and help them embrace change just as you have.

Indirect approaches will become less troubling and more of an exciting encounter when everyone on your side of the conversation is on the same page. The people you are closest to will enjoy the opportunity to share your story when they know with certainty that you are a fan of the story, too. Encourage them to share the details with enthusiasm. If you do, they won't hesitate to tell you about the conversations they have had, and you'll find excitement in learning how many people are interested to hear about your journey.

Later on, some individuals who approached your friend or family member before might come seeking to hear the story from you directly. This happens because they were so amazed by what they heard the first time that they have even more questions now. If and when this happens, take it as a positive outcome and keep their enthusiasm going.

Notes

____

____

____

____

SORROW

Some people will find your scars to be emotionally unbearable. If so, you'll notice a profound sense of sorrow within them. They feel sympathy for you and find it hard to fathom the damage that has been done to your appearance. They perceive that you are suffering a great loss. They worry about your misfortune and feel pain for your trials.

How have you responded to people who feel sorrowful for you?

____

____

____

____

Useful Tips: Recognize the devotion that is being expressed by the sorrowful person. When someone has a touch of compassion for you it's not a bad thing, although his or her interpretation of your situation might be entirely misconceived.

Attempting to console their emotions can be a delicate procedure. You might feel the urge to shut them off and dispel their condolences, probably because you don't want anybody to feel sorry for you. Maybe their behavior is creating an embarrassing public scene. Keep in mind that if you reject sympathy altogether, anyone paying attention can quickly count you as bitter and remorseful. There is a better way of communicating a sound message.

Be kind to the person. Assure them that you are okay, but also let them know that you sense a strong amount of goodness to them. The sorrowful person is expecting you to be sad and resentful. Kindness and gratitude are unexpected responses on your part that will leave them astounded.

Notes

____

____

____

____

WITHDRAW

Withdrawal is a reaction often found in tight corners when there is limited space. People can seem claustrophobic to scars. The many times I ride in public transit full of passengers narrate the situation well. It typically looks something like this:

I casually follow the line of people and make my way toward the back of the vehicle. As I go, each head looks up, each with the same baffled expression. Three words are seen on every forehead. *Don't. Sit. Here.* I feel vibes of recoil in every direction. Everyone would like to escape, but they can't. We're all strangers here, but this crowd sees me exceptionally different. A lady flinches when I accidentally brush her shoulder with mine. I quietly apologize. Focused, I take my seat. A child seated close by is staring. His mouth is gaped wide open, his eyes glued to my face in horror. His mother gives a scorn and quickly pulls the child away. The man sitting next to me gives a good long look before raising his newspaper to keep my face from view. No big deal, I think to myself. I'm totally used to this by now. I put my headphones on, turn the volume up, and give a long sigh. We ride on.

As someone with scars and a disfigurement, I have learned that there is no better tactic than to simply become accustomed to withdrawal. People will look away; they'll turn away and move away. Sometimes they'll flinch and run away. There are many reasons why they will choose to elude us, and all of them are normal. Often they sense fear, confrontation, embarrassment, lack of words, or shock.

What behaviors have you noticed when someone is withdrawing from you?

____

____

____

____

Useful Tips: You could guess which reaction these people are experiencing, but telepathy is not happening, so don't stress too much about what's going on. They are experiencing withdrawal. Allow them enough space to get a grip on their emotions. Continue on with your natural and well-composed self. Don't hide your personality or charisma. For most onlookers it will only take a minute to regain themselves. The rest will have to catch up to reality later on.

Notes

____

____

____

____

EMBARRASSMENT

A very common reaction people have is the feeling of embarrassment. They feel awkward and uneasy. They don't know quite how to approach you or what they should say. Normally, embarrassed people are more concentrated on themselves than on you because they are second-guessing their every move and word. They aren't educated on the implications of your scars, of where they came from and how they affect your life, and all of this mystery has them lost in insecurity.

How have you responded when people became embarrassed around you?

____

____

____

____

Useful Tips: As you become familiarized with the embarrassment that other people feel while in the presence of scars and disfigurement, recognize the value of being competent to facilitate to their needs. You can ease the uneasiness and give security to the insecure by being open and willing to talk about your differences and experiences. Don't expect everyone to have the courage to ask you questions. At the same time, don't think they are waiting for you to tell your personal eulogy. Most people only need enough information to know that you are not mentally or psychologically damaged and that you are able to communicate with them just fine. A cheerful attitude, a pleasant personality, and a willingness to discuss your story if needed are sufficient means to ending someone's reaction of embarrassment.

Two embarrassing scenarios to look at:

Scenario 1. One of your associates goes to great lengths to avoid being seen spending quality time with you. They're afraid of how their colleagues will judge them for being your friend. This can happen while on a date or at an outing with a co-worker. The associate surrenders the friendship at the moment they're caught with you at a public setting or private function. They ditch you on a fly and leave you behind as the obvious misfit.

Scenario 2. Someone speaks, saying something offensive or cross, like a joke or crude humor that's geared towards handicaps and disabilities. After they've spoken out loud, they awake to the impression that they have just offended you. They are now caught in an uncomfortable dilemma.

In both of these scenarios, who is the one with legitimate reason to be embarrassed, the other person or you?

Answer: There is no shame in being you. The offenders in these two examples are so self-conscious that they aren't even comfortable with themselves. They are exhibiting carelessness in how they treat other people. Don't let their actions cause you any grief. You know better than they do. They are embarrassed, and that's their problem. Their ignorance causes a huge privation for them, but you on the other hand are stalwart. Shrug it off, and move on.

Notes

____

____

____

____

FEAR

Fear is a reaction that will be expressed at various levels. Sometimes fear goes unnoticed. Other times a fearful person can act as though you are endangering their life by merely being there. One main cause for fear is the unavoidable fact that people will hear about our scars well before they are ever introduced to them. They are forewarned to expect something out of the ordinary. Unfortunately, their imagination has time to exaggerate the real image in advance. They go into the meeting with a premeditated hunch that we're ugly, different, and possibly terrifying.

How do you respond when someone shows fear towards your scars?

____

____

____

____

Useful Tips: There isn't anything you can do to silence the fear out of everyone or to prevent people from talking or hearing about you in advance. There are, however, two things you can do to reduce fear:

First, help the person feel relief by showing them you aren't as bad off or as "frightening" as they had envisioned. Be yourself. If they are afraid they are probably in defense mode. Don't get offended if they remain cautious, and don't be surprised if they become relaxed and warm up to you either. Next, begin immediately to build positive rapport with as many people as possible—even strangers and new acquaintances. In time, you will notice that instead of warning people about you in advance, they are talking you up with admiration.

Notes

____

____

____

DISGUST

It's nothing less than disappointing to find that people can be disgusted with your looks. When people react with distaste using loud and appalling declarations, they won't normally give heed to how cruel or obnoxious they're acting. At the moment, all they care about is letting you know that they find your appearance hideous and grotesque. Not only that, but your condition to them is absolutely awful. The longer they dwell on the thought of your scars, it seems the more repulsive you as a person become to them.

Has anyone ever acted with disgust towards you? If so, what did you notice about their behavior?

____

____

____

____

Useful Tips: When you can stand your ground while others show disgust it's nothing less than a testament of sheer strength. These are the times when the name-calling culprits come out to wreak havoc on one's self-esteem. If you tremble during their moment of mayhem, you will fall a heavy fall. You have the tools to prepare yourself for such times. Your opinions and what you know to be true about yourself are more powerful than anything someone can say, think, or even do to you. Their vision is limited, and yours is exceptionally keen.

Part of you being adequately prepared means that you already know how different people will react to you. You know what to expect. A piece of that learning process is memorizing the remarks that you will hear and the names that you will be called. Nothing anyone says should be a surprise.

Let the storms of disgust roll in. If you are convinced from head to toe, inside and out, that you are a rare case of awesomeness, then any vile winds of malice will blow on past you. Stand strong and keep your aim high.

Notes

____

____

____

____

RIDICULE

When a person or group uses speech or actions towards you with the intent of causing contemptuous laughter, mockery, harassment, vexation, or other forms of hurtful disturbance, they are purposely victimizing you. People that do this are the antagonists in the world of the scarred and disfigured. They are the bullies and the intimidators. They find pleasure in teasing and heckling. Don't downplay the fact that people who ridicule are capable of escalating the situation to the extent of causing physical harm. You need to know what steps to take in order to defend and protect yourself.

Useful Tips: Your safety is priority. Before you find yourself being targeted for ridicule, know who your resources are as well as where and how to reach them. Even the strongest champions of emotional strength need a place to turn when their safety is in jeopardy. Treat times of ridicule as emergencies even if you are certain that you are not at risk.

Although you are mentally stronger and wiser than any of your oppressors, there is absolutely no need to prove it to them. Prove it to yourself by getting out, avoiding conflicts, and by pressing on with resolution.

Name two sources of help that you can always contact in times of ridicule.

Name: ________________________ Phone number: _____________ Email:_________________

Name: ________________________ Phone number: _____________ Email:_________________

Notes

____

____

____

____

End of force #3

FORCE NUMBER FOUR: THEIR OPINIONS

Opinions are like clay. With patience, attention to detail, and creativity, they can be molded.

<u>Exercise:</u> Identify among these areas of life where the opinions of other people matter.

Job interviews	Advertisements	Marriage proposals
The courtroom	Religion	Essay tests
Athletics	Work resume	School classroom
Home and Family	Dating	Food Preparation
Fashion	Music and Art	Politics
Social Networks	Transportation	Sales
Parenting	Shopping	Friendships
Nature	Office and Work	Science

Other people's opinions are pretty much everywhere.

Now, one might say,

"I don't care what other people think."

Or

"People can have whatever opinions about me that they want, but that doesn't change who I am or the way I'm going to be."

Yes, your thoughts and opinions are priority, AND you shouldn't get offended by the opinions of other people, but don't deceive yourself. Just because your opinions are priority, that doesn't mean the opinions of others don't have a place at all. And don't forget, everyone's opinions are capable to change, even your own.

Together, we need to firmly believe in the possibility of perceptional change for everyone.

Society is better off when we help people change their opinions about scars and disfigurement. Change of this kind is accomplished by proving that we are capable, talented individuals who share the same potential as anyone else.

It was Gandhi, who said, *"As a man changes his own nature, so does the attitude of the world change towards him."*

Gandhi was right! I first experienced his rule of attitude change when I was thirteen years old. At that time, my family had moved to a new side of town, and I was struggling to survive the emotional challenges of school.

One day, after enduring an episode of intense criticism from some classmates, I found myself gazing out the window of the school bus, wondering if things were ever going to change. Normally, I would have doubted that they would, but that day—out of nowhere—a life-altering thought came to my mind. "I pledge to become the most popular kid with scars on his face that anyone has ever seen!" The words were a mixture of frustration and a determination to change my environment. And that day, those were the words I needed.

It might sound immature, but at that time popularity was a motivating factor for me. I was already attracting attention without even trying, but the attention was always negative. Perhaps if I were able to attract even more attention on a larger scale, for reasons other than my odd appearance, things would change for me. To achieve this goal, I needed to show that I was fun, adventurous, and entertaining. There was one stipulation: I could no longer feel sorry for myself. I had to demonstrate to everyone that I was happy with being me, happy being in my own skin. To sell this idea, I had to be one hundred percent convinced of it. For if I, or anyone else, didn't believe I was genuine, the idea simply wasn't going to work. This was the best scheme that had crossed my mind up to that stage of my life. At no point were my actions fake. By finally exposing who I was on the inside, for the first time, I would actually become a real person; I would bring that person to the surface and show the world who I really was.

Before the thought of being "the most popular kid with scars" came to me, I was already everything I said I was going to be. Underneath the scars I was fun, adventurous, and entertaining. I just wasn't good at magnifying those traits. I wasn't effective at helping other people see those qualities in me. But that became the area of life I was determined to improve. All I needed was that motivating factor—that original pledge to live differently.

Popularity was a short-term motivator. I grew out of that a long time ago. Today, what motivates me is completely different. Something else drives me forward now.

My current pledge says:

"I will make a difference in people's lives by successfully helping as many as possible overcome the obstacles of having scars and disfigurement."

You see, a pledge is a statement that declares what your *motivating factor* is. It's that thing that you put faith in and fight for. The sound of your pledge should fortify you and resonate within you. It is a personal, solemn expression of the person you know you are. Your pledge doesn't need to be of value to anyone else but yourself. It should be realistic, obtainable, and communicate your sincere ambitions and feelings.

Before starting a diet, an exercise routine, or any other kind of mind and body transformation, the person seeking change should have a clear idea of what they want to achieve. In a similar way, you and I should envision the persona we want to be at the end of our journey. That vision, that idea, that goal, affirms what you expect to achieve out of life. It is the guiding statement that will direct and challenge you along the way. It is your motto. By your pledge you will change your nature, and through this change the attitude of the world will change towards you, just as Gandhi said.

Design your pledge

Here are some examples of real pledges that might help you gain inspiration:

"When my children started asking what happened to make me look so different from other people, I knew I had to change my ways. There can't be anymore hiding. It's time to talk about what happened. My children and their children's children deserve to know that I am a survivor. I pledge to make my story heard."

"I pledge to not be afraid of how kids act towards me at school. My opinion is that I'm cool. I think my scars are cool, too."

"I have always wanted to be a teacher. I dream to inspire and educate others, but I have always feared being in front of groups. I want to influence people, but I have been concerned about what an audience will think about me. I can't allow that to stop me anymore. I pledge to be the teacher I dream to be. With or without these scars, I will become a teacher!"

"I pledge to not fear going into public. People can react to me however they want. I am grateful to be me and nothing that anyone can say or do will diminish that."

"When people ask what happened to me from now on, I pledge to always have a response ready for them, and I will be happy to share it. I will respect the curiosity of people and will be true to my experiences."

"I have suffered a great deal, but I have also learned a lot on how to be strong. One thing I battle with is reacting with envy. I often wish I could look like other people. I know that's not realistic. Despite the odds, I know I have much to do and still a lot to be excited for. I pledge to forsake envy and all negative opinions about myself."

“I pledge to think positively about my birthmark. I have learned to recognize it as a positive attribute of my unique life story. I will not be ashamed of being different, and I will help other people see that I am perfectly fine with it.”

“I always thought my scars were preventing me from getting the jobs I wanted. I blamed my scars for every failed job interview and every missed promotion. I believed that to be a leader you have to look like a leader. It was my attitude that was holding me back. A year ago I changed my attitude, and now I have the job I want. I pledge to maintain a positive attitude in the workplace.”

“I pledge to not stress about people's reactions to me. I know what to expect from them. I have been trained to be ready for anything. I am a rare case of strength!”

Now it's your turn. Design your pledge.

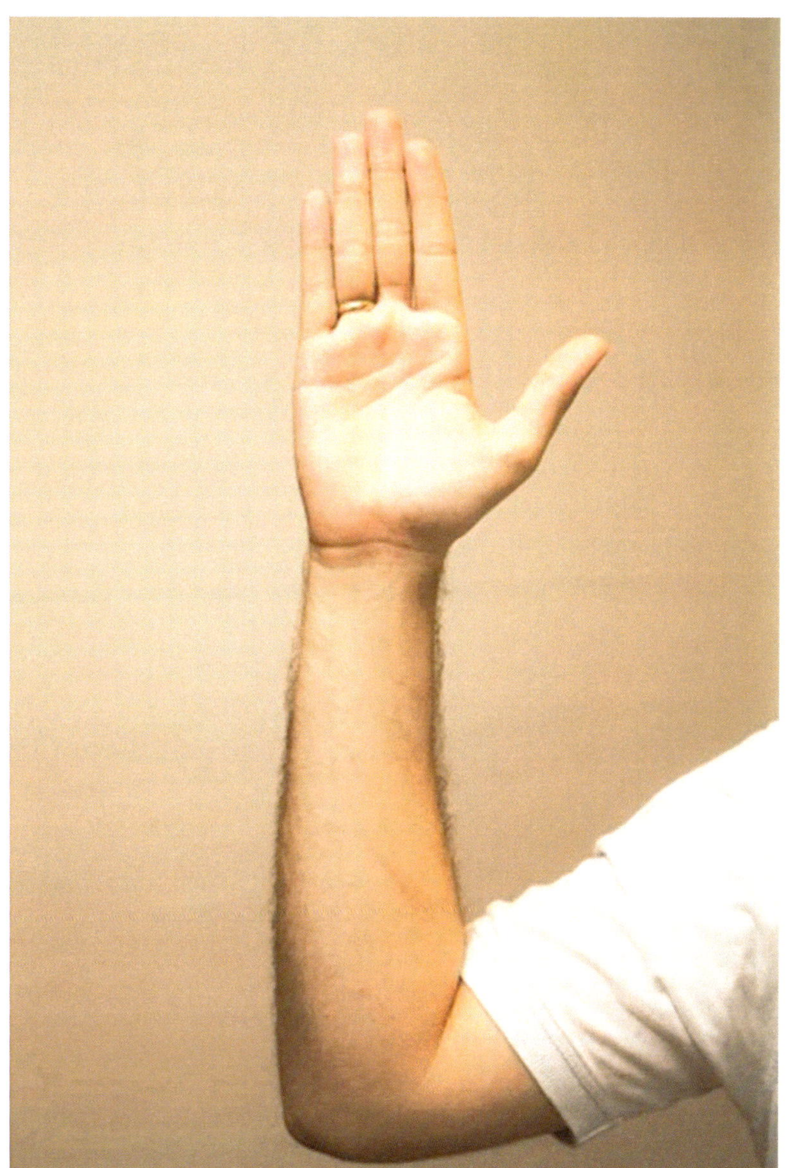

MY PLEDGE

____

____

____

____

____

Signed ____ Date_______________________

- **Frame this page and hang it in a place that you see every day.**
- **Live by it. Be true to it. Believe in it. Fight for it.**

Conclusion to the Four Forces

In this section we have explored four forces in depth. They are the forces of your reactions, your opinions, the reactions of other people, and the opinions of other people. These forces surround our everyday life.

As individuals with scars or a disfigurement, you and I are different. Experience has given us something unique. We can see and feel our differences, and so can other people. The objective established in this section is to cultivate a change of reaction and change of opinions to our scars from a negative outlook to a positive one, from a bad perspective to a good one. This happens when we accept and appreciate our scars as valuable additions to who we are. We cannot control every reaction or opinion, but we can be prepared and ready for them.

A fluent understanding of these four forces will prepare you for future plans, future obstacles, and all levels of social interaction. From this learning, greater knowledge of what to expect from a wide variety of situations has been explained.

When your reactions and opinions promote your own well-being and when you pledge to move forward, positive change takes place in other people as well. With time, the reactions and opinions that others have towards you can be molded to reflect your own.

THE PRIVATE SECTOR

The private sector encompasses the subdivision of life where you are alone. This includes your state of mind, your personality, habits, activities, and the condition of your independence when no one else is around.

Summary

When you are alone you can think and act for yourself to the extent of your circumstances without the input and interference of anybody else. This section called *The Private Sector* will direct you to incorporate enough time for yourself that you become familiarized and acquainted with who you are both internally and externally. Successful completion on this topic means you are in no way a stranger to yourself. You find contentment not only in having scars, but also in the ability to feel free and comfortable in every setting.

Finding Balance

Personalities differ extensively when it comes to finding peace with one's alone time. On one end of the pendulum are people who are always alone and who want to be left alone. These individuals are usually alone because they're eluding reactions and opinions from the public. They prefer being apart from society at all times. Seclusion is their solution, but it is not a healthy one. On the other end of the pendulum are people who have a very difficult time being alone at all. Without constant interaction, depression rapidly soaks in, and being with other people is an escape from a solitary prison. Neither extremity of this pendulum is where anyone should be. We need balance in this arena. Being alone should not be a recipe for depression, and no one should constantly be hiding out either.

In the middle of this pendulum is the luxury of temporary privacy. An emotionally healthy person normally spends solitary time doing and thinking things that aren't an emotional drag. This means they don't dwell on their abnormal looks or make their scars into an unnecessary predicament. When alone, we have the gratifying opportunity to enjoy our own interests completely out of sight. Alone time is an opportunity to dedicate energy to the enhancement of our interests and to the improvement of our talents. By doing these things we recognize that there's much more to who we are than what's on the surface.

To find peace with your inner self, you might have to break through several layers of mixed feelings that are combating with the way you look. Ask yourself if your scars make you unstable or agitated. Is it hard to consent to a future with scars? As with any new venture, you'll want to be emotionally and mentally prepared for what's ahead. When you decide that it's time to commence this odyssey, there are a number of things that will help you get started.

Take Time to Grieve

I was nineteen when my father unexpectedly died in a car accident. When it happened, I made the mistake of not allowing myself to properly grieve his death. For a period of time I didn't cry and didn't allow myself to get upset. Instead, I remained busy and chose to ignore my loss. Within a few days, I learned an unforgettable lesson: *Emotion is energy in motion.*

Energy, in the form of sadness and anger will build up exponentially if it is unable to flow out of the emotional nervous system properly. Because of my father's death and my unwillingness to grieve, the energy in my body eventually became like a shaken can of soda ready to burst. What was the result? Painful stomach ulcers and internal bleeding! My constrained emotions had amplified to the point of making me physically ill. Being sick was something I couldn't ignore. A wise physician ordered me to take adequate time for grieving. After all, I had experienced one of the greatest losses of my whole life! My body and mind were feeling it, but I wasn't expressing it, and now it was leading to bigger complications.

You have scars or are otherwise disfigured. With that said, you also need to admit that you have experienced a great loss. Something about your physical self is gone, or your life has changed in an unexpected and undesired way. You didn't plan on this happening, and now your whole environment has transformed.

Within you is the ability to cope with your losses. A key principle in coping is recognizing that there is a problem, so it's okay to miss the old you. It's all right to be very upset about what has happened. It's normal to be frustrated with your situation. Relief will come, but to get there you have to release all constrained energies and grieve properly when in pain.

Grieving is vital in order to proceed, so open up and grieve thoroughly. Let the energy move through and out of you. When the timing is appropriate, you will be able to climb out of grief mode. Periodically, you can revisit and grieve some more. Of course grief is an emotion that no one wants to retain interminably, but it definitely has its place in the healing process.

How does grieving help us emotionally?

____

____

____

____

____

____

How does grieving help us physically?

____

____

____

____

____

____

What has hurt you the most about your situation?

____

____

____

____

____

____

Why is it important to climb back out of grief mode?

____

____

____

____

____

____

Get Acquainted

In order to feel completely at ease, it's important for us to become so acquainted with our scars and physical differences that they will no longer be foreign objects to us. Don't delay in doing extensive research on yours. Spend enough time in front of the mirror to examine every aspect of them with intimacy, down to every color, shape, size and texture. A deep understanding of what you have and a close association with them is better than bypassing them. If you are ever curious to know more, or you require additional time to contemplate what you have, simply go back to expound on this practice. Get acquainted with yourself. Read more, learn more, ask more, and observe your scars more until your connection with them is sound.

Like any long-term relationship, the one you have with your scars or disfigurement will progress through different stages—from strangers to companions, through periods of bonding, to finally feeling as one.

Name five researched facts that are specific to your scars or disfigurement.

Example: My scars are extremely sensitive to both hot and cold temperatures.

1.____

2.____

3.____

4.____

5.____

Name three random facts about your scars or disfigurement that you have discovered on your own through mere observation.

Example: The scar on my back just happens to be in the shape of South America.

1.____

2.____

3.____

Kindle Hobbies

Everyone needs a favorite pastime to get past the hard times. Life might be thrown out of proportion after trauma strikes, but it doesn't have to stagnate. If you find you can no longer enjoy your previous hobbies, now is the perfect time to kindle new ones. The famous phrase, "When your dog dies, get a new dog" applies. Do something you've always wanted to do, or something you've never considered trying before. If you become bored with one activity, move on to the next. There are more hobbies to enjoy in this world than we'll ever have time for.

Stay motivated. One doesn't have to be the most proactive person in order to keep their motor skills active. Without regular activities of some kind, anyone can fall into a slump. Hobbies don't have to be fast paced or require heavy exertion. They range from very relaxing to physically intense. That's why hobbies are great. They're enjoyable activities that you alone choose to do.

Why is it important for us to have hobbies?

____

____

____

____

What are some of your current hobbies and how do they keep you motivated?

____

____

____

____

Try something new. Learning a new skill or a new ability is good for the brain. What new activity do you plan to try?

____

____

____

____

Scar Treatment

Incorporating scar treatment into your life is productive if the methods you choose are fit for your case and if they don't impinge on your standards. As examples, the use of cosmetics, prosthetics, camouflage, patches and surgery are viable options for many people, but they are not for everyone. Not everyone wants treatment, and not everyone needs it. There are treatment methods (like this course) that are strictly motivational and available to anybody. Deciding what kind of scar treatment to pursue, if any, is a highly personal matter, and for that serious discretion is advised.

The fundamental point of scar treatment is to make you feel better about yourself and more at ease with your appearance. Unfortunately, many individuals end up finding that they invest too much time, exertion, and monetary means into eliminating or covering something up that they know will ultimately never go away. Others use caution and evade disappointment before even starting down this path.

If you have scars or disfigurement that you know right now will ultimately never go away, know that it is possible to keep the scars and still treat the emotional symptoms of wanting them gone.

Allow me to reveal the best and most effective alternative method to scar treatment: Personalized and professional mentoring.

The Role of a Mentor

A major inconvenience that comes with having scars and disfigurement is that practically no one around you is able to relate to the obstacles you have to deal with. Close alliances like family and friends are naturally supportive, but until someone is able to climb into your skin, they will never know how it is to be in your situation.

For most, the challenges that come with having scars demand an overwhelming amount of effort, patience, and long-suffering. The measurement of time, pain, and strife that one has to go through in order to successfully adjust and thrive again can be tremendous. This laborious undertaking is reduced substantially when someone who comprehends the situation firsthand is present and able to lead the way.

One of the best ways to learn any new ability is to spend time with an expert. A mentor is someone who has already acquired the skills or talents that you're seeking. Not only are they willing to assist, a mentor also possess a rare eagerness to share their wisdom, experiences, and knowledge. They're anxious to see their mentee grow and develop into the person that they aim to be.

A good mentor can honestly say that they know what you're going through. They have their own story that can relate to yours, and they are prepared to give the best advice and suggestions modified to your specific case. Guidance from a mentor is offered under a low-pressure, self-discovery approach and addresses the issues in life that matter most.

Mentorship can focus on various topics, including overcoming emotions, dealing with people, getting back to work, excelling in school, establishing relationships, learning to forgive, or reaching short and long-term goals. A mentor knows what it takes to accomplish these things because they have already done so for themselves. They want to share what they know and are awaiting the opportunity. If you have not seriously contemplated the role that a mentor can play in your life, it is highly encouraged that you do. No one should go the difficult journey alone. A personal mentor is perhaps the most valuable of all resources available to you. Find one and put the tools and strategies they offer to use.

Conclusion to the Private Sector

The private sector encompasses the part of life when you're alone. If alone time is something you seldom have, you're encouraged to incorporate more of it into your lifestyle. We all need time to be alone so that we can explore our own thoughts and feelings without any external pressures or constraints.

Find emotional balance within the luxury of temporary solitude. Allow yourself the opportunity to overcome all anxieties and fears of having a visible difference. Take time to grieve your physical losses. Let your emotions flow through and out of you. When appropriate, climb out of grief mode. Take time to become intimately acquainted with your scars and overall appearance until you feel as one with them. Kindle your hobbies. Stay motivated by enjoying amusement, recreation, and by trying new activities.

Scar treatment comes in many forms. Explore your options. Be proactive in finding which method, if any, is best for you.

Work with a personal mentor. An expert who has already achieved what you want is capable and available to guide you to those results.

THE PUBLIC SECTOR

The public sector encompasses the part of life where you are in the midst of other people.

Summary

Scars and disfigurement can make facing the public a daunting experience. From small groups to large crowds and in virtually every public setting, we are planted within a spectrum of human interactions, engagements, and various levels of interpersonal communication. All of that noise can leave a heavy strain on one's courage, as it is unarguably intimidating to deal with. Nonetheless, coping with the noise and commotion, and learning to associate and interact in the public is part of the growth process we all must undertake.

In this section we'll study how the world views scars and disfigurement from different perspectives. Existing barriers within society as a whole will be brought to your awareness, and we'll construct some of the bridges we all have to cross when we encounter gaps in societal understanding. In the end, you'll be equipped with knowledge and skills for entering the public as yourself, ready to take on the world.

World Views

Earlier in the book we discussed the influence that reactions and opinions have on everything, from our own emotions and behavior to how we coexist with other people. Let's dig a little deeper now. Let's talk about why some opinions, which carry major impact on our lives, are shared by society on a broad scale.

The Great Taboo

By definition, when something is prescribed as being improper and unacceptable by society, it is a taboo. Is it any surprise then, that in most parts of the world, society has placed a great taboo on physical scars and disfigurement? In most societies, scars and disfigurement have been deemed improper and unacceptable.

Human beauty is recognized around the world, and it has been since the beginning of mankind. The closer one's appearance gets to the world's view of beauty, the better off they are. By society's standards, the more beautiful one is, the more attractive they are to opportunities. On the flip side, the further away one gets from that ideal beauty, the more shunned and blackballed they become.

As individuals with visible differences, we know that we will be ostracized and treated unequally for how we look. With time we learn to expect that from people. We know that we will be treated as an isolated group, but we also know that the reasoning behind that isolation is conclusively meaningless.

If we were to trace mankind's behavior through the centuries, we see that fear and avoidance to physical differences has always been there. In the medieval period, for example, leprosy demonstrated how a disfiguring illness caused major distress in society during that time. The leper was shunned and cut off from society completely for the disease he carried and also for how he looked. Time shows us that anyone who is visibly different has always been interpreted as being unhealthy and out of place. What we see in present day behavior is no different; it is clearly a continuation and remnant of the same barbaric and ignorant behavior that has always existed. The natural man shuns the disfigured man. It's a subliminal part of his human psyche that is pretty much non-erasable.

Ridding the world of a taboo like this one is very hard to do. Man has tried rigorously to advance from his barbarian beginnings. Progress is evident since the medieval period. In recent decades, the decency of mankind has pushed to expunge bigotry and prejudice from society. Today, most people would struggle to give a public snub to someone based on their race, religion, gender, or sexual orientation, yet somehow the disfigured person is still shunned without any delay. Why is this? Are we to be the last sub-group of humanity to be seen and treated as equals? Based on historical trend, it may very well be the case. Meanwhile, we must learn to live, thrive, and prosper with this great taboo in our midst. We have no other choice. We must learn to prosper with the way things are, or we'll fail to succeed.

The modern day taboo that surrounds us also bleeds into other human behaviors that affect everyday life. Let's observe what some of those are.

Stereotypes

A stereotype is a commonly held public belief about specific social groups or types of individuals. Historically, race and culture have given rise to widely accepted stereotypes, where the party being singled out is typically degraded and placed into a cube of automatically shared traits with the whole group, all of which can be entirely fictitious or irrelevant to the individual.

Examples of existing stereotypes include:
Cowboys: Cowboys drive trucks, listen to country music, and wear boots.
Asians: Asians are good at mathematics, eat rice, and know martial arts.
Mexicans: Mexicans work for cheap, eat burritos, and have mustaches.
Blonds: Blonds are ditsy, gullible, and easily confused.
People with scars: People with scars are scary, sad, and mysterious.

As is evident in these examples, the target group becomes segregated and unfairly judged by collective opinion instead of by individual content.

Why are stereotypes such a big deal?

Stereotypes are a big deal for many reasons. One reason stems into something that we deal with every day: Popular culture.

Pop-Culture

Pop-culture feeds stereotypes. Scars and disfigurement have always had their place in literary pop-culture and entertainment. From the sideshow at a traveling circus to the television in the living room, a character's strange looks have always wrought fascination with the masses. Books, movies, comics, and stories have been created over the years where abnormal features of characters have caused hysteria among viewers. Often the dangerous villain has scars on his body or has a disfigured face. Scars in pop-culture are usually symbols of suffering and signify ugliness to spark fear in the audience.

Identify characters in pop-culture history that have affected the way people view and react to scars or disfigurement.

Character	Literary Work
Quasimodo	***The Hunchback of Notre Dame***
Two Face	***Batman***
(List Another Character)	**(Literary or Screen Work)**
(List Another Character)	**(Literary or Screen Work)**
(List Another Character)	**(Literary or Screen Work)**

Fact: The average person will place less trust in a stranger with a visible disfigurement than in a stranger without one.

The stereotype fed from pop-culture has managed to eclipse the stories and impact the real world in which we live and where we have to survive. This creates a long-term problem that revolves around one single element: *Trust*.

A good parent tells their child to never trust a stranger, but as we get older, strangers become part of our daily interactions. We trust strangers at the restaurant to cook our food, we trust strangers to fix our car at the mechanic shop, and we trust strangers at the bank to transact our finances. It's a fact that the average person will place less trust in a stranger with a visible disfigurement than in a stranger without one. If people are going to place less trust in you simply because you have scars or a disfigurement, then this obviously creates a problem.

What can be done to fix the barrier of trust?

1. Identify what people are assuming

2. Break the pattern

3. Gain trust

Identify what people are assuming about you. Think along the lines of the stereotype. Given the choice, why would someone prefer trusting a stranger who doesn't have a visible difference to you? Or would they?

Bring the question back to pop culture. Most people aren't going to consider you a dangerous villain just because you look different, but based on possible assumptions and the influence of a stereotype mindset, they might not trust you the way you'd hope.

Talk it out. What assumptions could a stranger have about you that would prevent them from placing less trust in you than in someone else?

Example: At first glance, people probably think I'm not a nice person. Maybe they think I'm sad.

____

____

____

____

Stereotypes lead to assumptions

The presence of a stereotype can lead people to make assumptions. One assumption that people regularly have is the idea that people with scars and disfigurement don't want to be approached or questioned about their differences.

Common assumptions are:

"That person looks like they're in serious pain."

"They look like they have major issues they're dealing with, so I won't bother them or make their life more complicated than it already is."

"Look at those weird scars! They look scary. I'd be willing to bet they have mental problems, too."

"Don't get too close to them, and don't point or ask questions, you'll only hurt their feelings."

"They seem nice, but they might not be physically capable to fulfill the tasks this job entails."

Break the pattern. When false assumptions are made about you, decisions of trust can easily impact your situation. For example, when job-hiring officers assume too much during interviews and job offers end up failing. Assumptions are why potential favors dissipate and chances for development dwindle. Regrettably, too many people are afraid to place trust in people with scars simply because of what they see at first glance. That's why it is crucial that we break the pattern of this stereotype so that it no longer applies to us.

We must break the pattern by *being* different.

What does the stereotype say about you as a person?

Answer: Based on the routine stereotype, as someone with scars or disfigurement you are probably scary, sad, or mysterious.

Is that all it says?

Answer: No. When we zoom in closer we learn that it says a lot more than that about who we are as people.

Activity

Try these questions on for size to get an idea of where you are in comparison with the stereotype. For each question, answer by circling “Always,” “Sometimes,” or “Never.”

How often do you shy away from telling people your story?	Always Sometimes Never
How often do you get embarrassed when asked what happened?	Always Sometimes Never
How often do you feel resentful about your differences?	Always Sometimes Never
How often do you hide from people?	Always Sometimes Never
How often do you avoid going into public?	Always Sometimes Never
How often do you avoid questions about your scars?	Always Sometimes Never
How often do you cover yourself up so that children can't see?	Always Sometimes Never
How often are you offended by insults?	Always Sometimes Never
Do you lack confidence around people that you find attractive?	Always Sometimes Never
Do you believe people without scars have advantages over you?	Always Sometimes Never
Do you use your scars as an unnecessary excuse for handouts?	Always Sometimes Never
Do you feel vulnerable when people talk about your scars?	Always Sometimes Never
How often do you wish your scars weren't even there?	Always Sometimes Never

This is the stereotype that people expect you to live up to. These are only twelve questions among a great many more that could be asked. They represent the pattern of behavior that we need to break. If you find that you always, or sometimes, do one or more of these things, then in those areas of life you are living the stereotype. You see, people expect you to do these things all of the time. They would never blame you for doing so. It makes sense and it's logical that insults would be offensive. It's within reason that you would avoid confrontation and curiosity. It would be no surprise to anyone if you don't get very far in life or achieve very much since there are so many challenges holding you back.

In order to live differently and have different outcomes, we have to be different. The answer to every one of these questions should be a powerful "Never." Only when we completely stop living up to the expectations of the stereotype will the pattern be broken.

Gain trust.

Trust levels should not be weighed on whether or not someone has scars or a disfigurement. Good looks and appearances should not be requirements for establishing trust either, but whether they *should* or not doesn't apply. The fact is, people assume things all the time based on what they see, and the consequences of that are ours to deal with.

In the beginning, people see us differently. That is normal and natural. What they see next is up to us.

We have to believe that being different is a good thing and that being seen differently is, too. It is what we do with our "differences" that makes all the difference in the world. At the moment when people learn that we are unique AND trustworthy, we eradicate the stereotype and jump ten thousand paces ahead!

When the pattern of the stereotype is broken, we leverage ourselves and gain people's trust. Trust is important. Trust is the ticket to opportunity. With trust we're considered capable. With trust we're regarded as confident, and with trust we're seen as being driven.

When trust is gained, the following characteristics will be evident:

T - Thoughts	**People will think and perceive, based on your behavior, that you are living an emotionally healthy life.**
R - Recognition	**People will recognize your efforts to succeed. You're ambition and enthusiasm will be noticeable.**
U- Understanding	**People will understand that your scars are not a burden for you.**
S - Self-reliance	**People will know that you have confidence in yourself.**
T - Taking action	**People will take action. They will approach you and entrust you with opportunities.**

Hollywood Scars

Entertainment and media have a huge influence in the public sector. Mass opinions, worldwide ideas, traditions, and political movements are affected by messages driven by television, radio, and the Internet. A lot of what people do is based on what they are fed through media and entertainment sources.

When was the last time you watched a movie where the main actor or actress had a visible disfigurement or scar that was not makeup or a special effect? Talk shows highlight guests with scars and disfigurements all the time, but have you ever spotted a talk show host who has one of their own? Have you ever seen a news anchor with plainly visible scars or a bizarre disfigurement? Has it dawned on you that people on the front line of public media and in the entertainment world don't commonly have scars or disfigurements on display? Over time Hollywood and the media have proven themselves reliable to perpetuate a stereotype that should be eliminated. Why is this the case?

Here are a few reasons why they do:

First impressions: The first thing an audience sees directly impacts their tendency to either keep watching and remain focused or turn away and lose interest. If what the audience sees makes them uncomfortable they are not likely to stay connected.

Reputation: There are two halves to Hollywood and big media. One half is the act; the other half is the critic. Both halves equal one large exchange. The act is everything that is given to the audience in the form of visual and audible product. The other half, the critic, is the response of the audience. The critic defines the product's reputation, and a product without a strong reputation is nothing.

Image: As part of a visual product, each person contributing to a form of entertainment or media outlet has a duty to fulfill. Part of that duty is retaining a specific image. If it is believed that someone doesn't fulfill their duty, a way is found to weed them out in order to continually sell the product.

First impressions, reputation and image all carry massive consequences weighing on the success or failure of an entertainment or media product. Corporations take huge chances whenever they extend an opportunity to an individual with an image that might bring outcomes that they are unsure about. For these reasons we don't see many scars or disfigurements in Hollywood and big media, which is a very influential area of life.

Let’s review.

Why are scars and disfigurement particularly uncommon in Hollywood and media outlets?

____

____

____

____

The future of scars in entertainment, media, and pop-culture

If more people with scars and disfigurement had public roles in television, media, and show business, do you expect there would be a positive impact on society? Imagine if it were common to see physical differences on television regularly. Would audiences grow more accepting of abnormal appearances? Would the stereotype we're dealing with be more or less potent over time?

These are questions that make a great discussion. The argument, of course, goes both ways. While many perceive that there aren't enough scars and disfigurements in the public eye, others firmly believe that a gradual increase of them would make every one of us victim to additional scrutiny.

What do you think? Should more people with scars be seen in Hollywood and mainstream media? Why or why not?

____

____

____

____

The Innocence of Children

Young children are vulnerable to the influences of the society that surrounds them. They have a natural gift of innocence, but they can also be quick to act obnoxious, rude, and to bellow hideous insults. Children enjoy asking questions, experimenting with one's emotions, and they like to test their limits. Sometimes our scars or abnormal looks are what trigger disruptive behavior in them.

A couple years back I paid a visit to some acquaintances from work at their home. The reason for the meeting was professional. I had business on the brain that afternoon and had left all personal affairs behind. Not long after arriving and having barely started in discussion, came the abrupt entry of curious blond-haired children appearing out of nowhere.

"Hey, mister, what's that on your face?" one of them interrupted as he swarmed in.

"Yeah, what is that? Mom, do you see his face? He looks weird," another said, joining in while bouncing on the couch hysterically.

"Don't be rude!" their dad retorted. "All of you leave him alone and be gone! Go to your rooms right now!"

Disappointed, the children scurried off down the hallway out of sight.

"I'm so sorry!" the mother begged. "I hope they didn't offend you."

My response was both a relief as well as a surprise to these parents who were at that point beyond embarrassed. "Is it all right if your children come back in?" I asked with a grin.

"Come back in?" asked the wife, with a look of confusion across her face.

"Yes. If they may, I'd like to answer their questions and tell them my story."

"Are you sure about that?" asked her husband. His eyes were shooting back and forth between her and me.

"Absolutely!" I replied. "Nothing would give me more joy right now than to entertain their curiosity with a story that I'm sure they'll find interesting. It won't take more than a minute. Please invite them in."

The children were beckoned by their father and back within seconds. I put my notebook aside, scooted to the edge of the couch and leaned forward so they could get a closer look at the scars. The four boys and their sister were beyond fascinated to hear what I had to say. Their ears were glued to every word, and their eyes were as wide as headlights. Do you know what else I found most interesting? The parents showed equal, if not more attentiveness. In fact, both the mother and father each had several questions for me at the end. I found that very amusing.

The Lesson

A powerful sense of joy can be felt when we become involved in the purpose of education. By opening young minds, we can fill them with useful information for life.

Storytelling rarely takes more than a couple of minutes. In this instance, the children returned to their activities, but were satisfied to have learned something from me. Had I not shared with them, they would have been frustrated and also confused as to why their parents were chastising them for asking a visitor an innocent question. Parents are generally polite, but children frankly aren't as careful. Children carry a sharp sense of curiosity and boldness to them that should be admired more than anything else. They might be loud and reckless, but that can be overlooked.

I could tell you about other situations where I failed to extend an invite to hear my story. There have been many occasions when the parents controlled the situation their way. Parents tend to reinforce the stereotype that we're trying to break. Too many teach their children to bury their questions and to avoid real, solid answers. Real gratification never comes by turning curious children away. I have seen their disappointment when the information they want is shut down. All a child typically wants to know about one's scars or disfigurement is what happened to cause it. They might ask if you're in pain and if the scars will ever go away, but are those really such bad questions? Not really. When we have the guts to give an honest and inspirational answer, the world of a child transforms.

What good comes from sharing your story with children?

Example: Children will learn that it's not bad to ask questions. They learn that scars are normal.

____

____

____

____

What does sharing your story with the child teach the parent?

Example: The parent learns that I'm not embarrassed or ashamed to talk about my differences.

____

____

____

____

All-Knowing Adults

Last week I was at the bank when a child in line pulled his mother by the purse and asked, “What's on that man's face?” The mother, embarrassed to find what he was pointing at, scooped him up and whispered in his ear. “It's not nice to point, sweetie. The man was burned.”

I was in church when I noticed a young girl a few rows ahead of me ask her mother, “What's that red thing on that guy's cheek?” The mother took a quick glance back at me and then turned her daughter around. I read her lips as she said, “It is a birthmark, honey.”

Today while waiting in line at the supermarket, a young boy asked his dad, “Do you see that guy? What is wrong with him?” The father responded to his son as he paid the cashier. “Leave him alone, son. He was obviously in an accident or something." He then looked back at me and apologized for his son's remark.

"He was burned," they have said.

"He was in an accident," they say.

"It's a birthmark"—wrong again.

I've heard every possible answer from parents. While they're trying to correct the child's behavior they simultaneously avoid an uncomfortable conversation with me. A parent is not going to know that my scars are from a rare case of chickenpox unless they are already familiar with who I am. Honestly now... a rare case of chickenpox...how would they know?

This is funny about parents. Most of them prefer guessing or giving the wrong answer to their kids instead of allowing them to ask the uncomfortable question. Personally, I don't chase every family down after church to give the correct information. I don't always butt in at the supermarket to rectify the conversation, but I do speak up when I feel it is necessary.

Many have learned that I am fairly protective of my story and won't hesitate to give anyone the accurate version of it. Legitimately, I want parents to know what happened to me, and I'd rather their children know the truth instead of a lie, so often I open my mouth and share.

You might likewise overhear parents or other adults taking guesses at you, estimating the origin of your scars in isolated conversations. Too bad they don't have the courage to ask. They think they are being polite. That's why it's important to have tolerance with parents and their children, especially when you repeatedly hear the wrong explanations of your story being told over and over.

Things to keep in mind with parents:

- Parents are generally intimidated and too embarrassed to ask you what happened, especially at the spur of the moment.

- Parents are usually uncomfortable when a child creates a scene. When they're asked an awkward question about a stranger, they'd rather flee the situation than educate their problem child.

- It's much easier for a parent to quickly make up a story or to give a one-line remark to quiet their child than it is to talk to you.

What do you do in this situation? Do you prefer to leave it alone and allow the parent to educate the child with a blatant lie? Do you sit back and listen as they guess, or do you step in and speak up? There is no right or wrong reaction. You have the choice and the ability to speak your case whenever and if ever you decide.

To find what's best for you, give each way a try and record what you experience.

Scenario 1: A child asked their parent what happened to you. In response, the parent gave the child a false or incomplete answer. You decided to leave it alone and didn't say anything to them.

What did the child ask about you or what did they say?

____

____

____

How did the parent respond to the child?

____

____

____

What did you learn from this experience?

____

____

____

Scenario 2: A child asked their parent what happened to you. In response, the parent gave the child a false or incomplete answer. This time you decided to politely speak up and correct them with the real story.

What did the child ask about you or what did they say?

____

____

____

How did the parent respond to the child?

____

____

____

What did you say and do to correct the story?

____

____

____

What did you learn from this experience?

____

____

____

____

Conclusion to the Public Sector

This sector of life transcends the independent you and addresses major, worldwide influences affecting society as a whole.

Stereotyping, a behavior that derives much of its problems from pop-culture, shapes mass opinions. People are lead to make assumptions and to place less trust in individuals with visible differences, but we have the ability to break the stereotype and gain trust with people regardless of what society teaches.

HOME AND FAMILY LIFE

You are not the only one with scars. Everyone in your family has them, too.

Summary

Life at home among family is generally where we are most emotionally attached. It doesn't matter how often we are at home, or how close we are to family members. We're attached to family by either blood or adoption and that connection fills all the gaps.

For purposes of this course, the home will be defined as the place where each of us resides. Because life is unique to each of us, the words "home" and "family" can mean many different things. Not everyone is raised in one home, and not everyone resides in one place. There are single person families and families by the multitude. We're all different, so to incorporate the lessons of this section to your life, adapt the words "home" and "family" to match your own situation and needs.

Whether you experienced trauma, or if your scars are from birth, the scars that resulted from those events were not given to you alone. Family becomes scarred together. The effects of scarring and disfigurement can be as finite as airwaves. The sound of crisis is something that resonates not only within the halls of the home, but also within the chambers of every heart living there.

Total family recovery is possible, but it requires group effort and participation by every member. The vehicle that will drive a family forward is transparent communication. No one in the family can be left stranded, and everyone has an equal voice.

For the family to succeed, there has to be an understanding that although single members carry scars, they have been entrusted under the keep of the whole clan. The family should be a fellowship with a united purpose: To live a life with scars together and to obtain fulfillment as a household.

The Family Model

I was born into what can be called a traditional family model. My parents were married. My father was a business owner, my mother a homemaker. Together they had eight children, I being the fourth in line and first-born son. As siblings, we're composed of four sisters and four brothers. Although we are a traditional family model, we were never, however, “the perfect model family.” Together we had to learn the same exact lessons that families of other sizes and models learn.

Families of every kind have certain attributes in common when scars and disfigurement are present in the home. When one or more members of the family experience something traumatic, every member of the family is affected by it in their own personal way. The affects bring challenges that have to be reconciled with, and each member of the family plays a separate role while the challenges are faced together.

Scars carry over from generation to generation. Eventually, I grew up and left my parent's home. My siblings and parents are still connected to my story, but now I have children and a wife who have become appendages to the story. Because their father and husband has scars, new challenges will surely come that we'll face together. In this sense, scars are multi-generational.

In the next segment we will get an overview look at some of the challenges that scars can bring into a home.

Jen's Story

During a two-hour shuttle ride to the Las Vegas airport, a friendly and charismatic gal named Jen entertained me with a hurricane of questions. She and her fiancé, Stephen were on their way to the Florida coast for spring break. They were an enthusiastic couple, personable, and very talkative.

While verifying some documents on my laptop, Jen's energetic voice popped over my shoulder. “Hello, sir! I don't mean to be rude, but I couldn't help noticing your scars. You know, the ones on your face. Can you tell me what they are from?” She wasn't shy…not at all.

“Oh, no need to worry,” I replied. “Trust me, I don't find your curiosity rude. I'll be right with you and will be happy to give you the rundown of what happened.”

“Awesome!” she said, beaming. “I didn't mean to interrupt if you're busy. I'm usually not that direct, but your scars reminded me of some that my older brother has. He experienced an electrical burn at work in 2001.”

I quickly closed out the program on my computer and turned around to listen. Jen continued to give her fiancé and me the account of her brother, James. An accidental burn at his work had impacted their whole family. James was burned while working near damaged electrical cables at a construction site. Jen didn't understand exactly what had happened to him, but as his sister she was very alert to how he had been suffering ever since.

“His scars aren't that bad,” she explained. “But no matter how much we tell him that, he doesn't listen. He won't go back to work, he refuses to look for another job, and he is convinced that no girl will ever see anything in him now. He has pretty much given up!”

“I don't get that,” Stephen muttered as he glanced out the window. “James is an attractive guy. Why is he letting that one experience ruin the rest of his life?”

Jen sighed. “I don't get it either, and that’s not all that bothers me. My parents are suffering along with him. Not for the way he looks, they just long for the old James, you know? We would all like to see him return to his old self. He used to be really into athletics and would laugh and crack jokes all the time. We'd like to see him do the things he used to do, but he doesn't anymore. The truth is, when he was burned, everything changed. We've been here visiting him these last few days, and the whole time I was thinking to myself, 'gosh how I miss my brother.’”

Jen looked at me and apologized. I could tell she was deeply hurt by her brother's circumstance. Stephen was holding her hand. With a crooked smile he looked up at me and said, “You look like you've been through something too, bud, but you also look like you're carrying on just fine. Do you have any tips for us so that maybe we can help Jen's brother out a bit?”

“I wasn't burned like he was, but I do have a few pointers,” I answered. “I'm happy to help in any way I can.”

For the duration of the trip, Jen and Stephen bounced questions toward me. Jen was very relieved to talk to someone who understood. She was able to release her emotions and exchange them for an intake of newfound knowledge. She went away from that conversation knowing she could do her part in helping not only her brother James, but her parents and herself, too. Stephen also went away with an understanding. He found he had a role to play and was impressed to know that he could assist his soon-to-be wife as well as the whole family.

We discussed a lot of things during that shuttle ride. Of course everyone's situation is different, but some key topics that were talked about then can be applied to all of our lives.

Everyone in the family has scars

In this story, James was the one with physical scars caused by a traumatic, accidental event at work. The experience had obviously changed his life forever. By the sound of his reactions he was suffering badly, and by his opinions, he had lost all hope.

James' condition had also scarred the whole family. Everyone was feeling pain for him. By wondering if and when he would recover, they were each wondering if they themselves would, in turn, be able to do the same. Jen wanted her brother to be himself again. She wanted him to be the happy, funny, athletic brother she grew up with. She also wanted her parent's lives to improve. She saw the weight of worry that they were carrying and didn't like it. Jen also wanted to stop worrying herself. The sight of my scars not only reminded her of her brother's condition, the scars on my face reminded her of the whole family's situation.

Stephen, a soon to be addition to the family also became scarred by James' experience in his own way. When he witnessed his sweetheart disclose her emotions, he realized that if things were to get better, he had a role to play. Stephen wanted to help James so that in turn he could help Jen.

Do you see how everyone in the family has scars?

Think about your own situation now. You may be the one with the physical scars like James, or you may be a member of the family like Jen or Stephen. Whichever position you are in, recognize your scars for what they are. They might be on the surface, or they might be strictly emotional. Once you recognize what scars you have, take a minute to acknowledge what each of your family members is dealing with.

Right now, are you able to accurately decipher the emotional scars that each member of your family is dealing with?

Most people are unaware of the internal suffering that is being felt by one or multiple members of their own family.

Common emotional scars that are found within a family are:

Worry	**Concern**	**Fear**	**Sadness**	**Anger**
Embarrassment	**Stress**	**Guilt**	**Shame**	**Responsibility**
Panic	**Hopelessness**			

Learning about the emotional scars that each member of your family has is probably going to require some conversation between you and them. There is no point in guessing how they feel.

This brings us to the vehicle that will drive a family forward:

Transparent Communication

Transparent communication is the sharing of information that someone needs in order to understand what is going on at the time that they need it.

For a family to have unity there has to be transparency in the way that it communicates. What is a family without unity? A family without unity is a family divided. If our mind does not know the pains of our feet, how will it know to tend to them? Without knowing the struggles of our family members, we won't know how to tend to them either.

Consider the following family conversations:

"I learned from my father that he was feeling perpetually guilty for my accident. He believed it was his fault that I became disfigured and has been unable to forgive himself. Now that we're on the same page I can show him that he doesn't need to feel that way anymore."

"When we finally spoke, my sister admitted that she was embarrassed of me. She said she never wanted her friends to be around me because she was afraid they would value her less just because I look different. Since we've spoken she acknowledges that it's silly to be embarrassed over something like that. She has agreed to change her ways."

"My son has felt responsible for my happiness. Because my scars are from domestic violence, he is awake to the fact that I have a hard time trusting people. He took it upon himself to stand up for me and constantly assure me that people weren't out to cause me harm. This emotional response on his part has been incredibly stressful for him. I told him how much I appreciate him and I promised to be less of a burden."

It takes mutual effort for family members to come to terms and admit these kinds of feelings to each other. It isn't fun to hear these things. It's discomforting, and it's troubling. At the same time, this kind of conversation hammers out layers of built up ice and creates a renewing opportunity in the family. Be willing to listen and be open to the honesty of your family members. Whichever emotions are expressed together will surely reflect normal and natural feelings.

Freeing our emotions and communicating transparently among family is a necessary step to building the union that we want to exist within our most valued relationships.

Activity

Engage in transparent conversations with your family members. Learn the emotional scars that each one has in connection to your scars or disfigurement and begin to work them out together.

Family Member #1– Name____

What emotional scars does this family member have?

____

____

How will you work these things out together?

____

____

Family Member #2– Name____

What emotional scars does this family member have?

____

____

How will you work these things out together?

____

____

Family Member #3– Name____

What emotional scars does this family member have?

____

____

How will you work these things out together?

____

____

Family Member #4– Name____

What emotional scars does this family member have?

____

____

How will you work these things out together?

____

____

Family Member #5– Name____

What emotional scars does this family member have?

____

____

How will you work these things out together?

____

____

Conclusion to Home and Family Life

When one member of the family is scarred physically, everyone else is scarred emotionally in their own individual way. A family seeking unity should exhibit transparency in communication. The more awareness one member has to the pains and challenges of the rest of the clan, the more they will know how to help each other overcome every family obstacle.

SOCIAL LIFE AND FRIENDSHIPS

Under any circumstances, a true friend will defend the liberties we have to both be ourselves and to believe in ourselves.

Summary

What is a friend to you? Think about it. What defines a friendship and how does a real friend act and react to you having scars? With the accruing of social media, the word "friend" is increasingly being over used. Nowadays a list of friends might include people you have never met before and know very little about. That definition of "friendship," however, is precisely what friends are not.

Friends are whom we cling to for support. In this section, we'll take a detailed look at how friends can be assets for us as we encounter the social world. Being social is a large part of life, and therefore, fostering genuine friendships is something we should all learn to do. Of course, identifying someone as a genuine friend can be somewhat tricky. Many friendships are cut short, others end abruptly, and some simply lose their value over time.

We can learn to garner friendships that survive. We can learn to attract them and we can learn to identify them. We find that when friends promise to stick together no matter what, despite any differences they may have, if they hold true to that original promise, the bonds linking their friendship together grow stronger over time.

Isaac's Story

Several years ago I met a teenager named Isaac through his grandmother. Gail was her name. She and I were working the closing shift at a transportation depot at the time. Gail was a very caring woman. She was elderly and polite. She was alert to the fact that small deeds go a long way, and she did them constantly. I remember returning to my desk from running an errand one night and finding she had cleaned my entire workstation, computer, monitor and everything. I had only been gone maybe two minutes.

Upon my return, I looked over and found her reading a book and acting as though nothing had happened. "Gail, did you clean my desk while I was away?" I asked.

She didn't answer.

Did she even hear me? I wondered. Whatever she's reading has her completely absorbed. "Thank you for cleaning my desk, Gail. I really appreciate it!" I shouted loudly.

She looked up. "Yes, I did clean it. I'm sorry, Brady. Does that bother you?"

"No, it doesn't bother me. Sorry I'm such a sloppy desk jockey!" I replied sarcastically.

"Oh, you're not sloppy" she muttered, her eyes still glued to the book. "I just thought it m...mm...might help." She mumbled so fast the words were almost indistinct.

I sat down and began reviewing the next day's roster, but couldn't help noticing how nervous she was acting. Through the corner of my eye I could see her fidgeting. Her fingers were tapping on the edge of her table, and she appeared to be digging her eyes through the pages of that book as if she were looking for a clue of some kind. Whatever it was, it was very important.

I couldn't concentrate, so I slid my chair over in her direction. "Is everything all right, Gail?" I asked.

"Oh! What's that? Am I all right? Actually, Brady, not really. No, it's not a good night for me to be working. I'm really anxious to get home."

"What ya reading?" I asked softly. "Is it any good?"

"Yeah...it is" She replied. She bit her lip and after a slight pause, closed the book shut and set it on the table. "Brady, can I ask you something that might sound random?"

"Absolutely, Gail. I'm all ears. What's up?"

She spoke slowly. “The scars on your face... do they bother you?”

“Wow, that is a random question. Don’t worry though. They don't bother me. Not anymore anyway. Why do you ask?”

“This book I'm reading is about a family that survived a near fatal car accident. I'm reading it because my fourteen-year-old grandson and a group of boys from church were also in a severe accident while on their way to scout camp this summer.”

“Really?” I said in surprise. “That's awful! Is he okay?”

“By miracle, everyone survived, but it was a pretty bad accident. The van he was riding in went out of control and rolled over. Isaac, my grandson, came away with some broken bones and a large laceration on his face from a broken window. I'm worried about him because on Tuesday he's starting at a new school, and well, you know how teenagers can be. Of course, Isaac's afraid of what the other kids will say about his new scar.”

“Wow, that is incredible!” I said in amazement. “I'd like to meet Isaac someday. I can tell you from my own experience that a facial scar like his can have its share of social setbacks, but it's not the end of the world. He can still learn to make good friends.”

“I'm just grateful everyone survived,” she continued. “I know he'll be fine physically, but there are definitely challenges ahead of us. I'm raising him by myself, and I know him very well. I can tell he's emotionally impacted by all of this, not only by the accident, but also because he looks different. That kind of thing doesn't go away. He's young and has his whole life ahead of him. I'm afraid that over time he'll be more and more disappointed by his appearance and confused on how to handle it.”

By this point Gail was nervously trying to organize her thoughts. I could see she was deeply worried. Not only for Isaac. She also wanted to fulfill her role in helping him plan and prepare for a future with his scars.

After contemplating their predicament for a moment, I spoke up. “Gail, let me ask you something. Do I give you the impression that I'm bothered by the scars on my face?” I asked rather directly.

“Well, no.” She said hesitantly. “But I am curious to know how you deal with it.”

“After hearing that story you shared, I thought you would like to know,” I replied. “Let me tell you some of the things I've done that have helped me along my way. Maybe my ideas can help Isaac, too.”

"Ooh, I'd like that," she said with a deep sigh. She appeared to be somewhat relieved.

"Much like him, I also had to confront school and friends with a facial disfigurement. I had to look myself in the mirror, hold my head up and face my peers. I had to carry on, fight for what I wanted, and learn to be who I wanted to be, despite what other people thought of me. And guess what? I'm still in the middle of that process."

Gail raised her hand slightly to insert her opinion. "Brady, you are working a steady job, you have a wife and family, and you still have a lively sense of humor. Look at you! You have a positive outlook on life. That is exactly what I want for Isaac."

"Yes" I insisted. "But youth is hard enough as it is. As you can imagine, it's even more difficult when you have visible differences like ours. I grew up in a similar situation as him. It has been a long journey, but yes, I guess I have learned to carry on quite well. That's why I'm more than happy to tell you how I did."

I shared a lot of information with Gail that evening. So much, in fact, that I was guilty of distracting us from the job we were there paid to do. After work, she invited me to visit her and Isaac at their home in the near future. Being the super grandmother that she was, Isaac would have all the help he could get. I gladly agreed to the invite, and we set a date for the meeting.

Looking back on those visits, I realize Isaac wasn't as bad off as his grandmother had made him out to be. Gail was far more shook up from the accident than he was. Isaac had been through something traumatic for sure, but he was still a bright and determined kid. He had the charisma that any fourteen-year-old should have. Sure, he had the scars, and they were exactly as his grandmother had described, but he wasn't surrendering, nor was he going to let this car accident get in his way forever.

One thing Isaac was lacking was a strong support network of friends to stick by him as he pushed on at a new school. He hadn't been in contact with many of his friends since before the accident and would now be surrounded by new kids.

Undeniably, what Isaac, you, I, and anyone else with a visible difference needs is lasting friendships to support them in their determination to succeed. The following lesson is an excerpt of the things we discussed.

The Making of Friends

Maintaining genuine friendships is no meager accomplishment. It has been said time and again that family is forever, but friends come and go. Although this statement might be true for some, it isn't the case one hundred percent of the time. If we work at it, there is no reason why our friendships can't also remain forever intact. Some friendships have even been said to carry a sentimental value that equals, or surpasses that of family.

Making and keeping true friends can be difficult, especially when you have something that distinguishes you apart, like a scar or disfigurement, but it is nowhere near impossible. To get started, do the basic things that anyone has to do. You're not exempt from the normal patterns of a social life just because you look a certain way, so begin with the following basic activities:

- Spend time around people. You can't expect to make friends if you are constantly alone.
- Find people with common interests. Join clubs, organizations, or charities of interest in order to surround yourself with people who share the same hobbies.
- Talk with people. Make comments in group settings. Let people see your ability to articulate your thoughts and opinions openly. Talking helps people see beyond the surface of your skin and into your personality.
- Be personable. Make eye contact when you speak. Show interest in the lives of other people by asking them basic life questions and by being willing to answer any questions they may have for you. Never get offended by their questions.
- Don't wait for others to approach you. Take initiative by showing that you can be outgoing. Extend invitations. Show your interest in continuous relationships by inviting people to join you in the activities that you enjoy. If you're turned down, let them continue on their way. The right people will accept your offer and will stay.
- Don't pressure people into friendship. Tagging along and being someone's shadow probably isn't the best way to approach people. True friendship comes naturally. There is no point in forcing anyone into being your friend.
- Be a good friend to others. Show your loyalty by being there when things aren't going well for someone. A shallow friend leaves when times get tough. Being a true friend means you are the one they can lean on for support.

Most people find that friendships are eventually won when they follow and repeat these simple guidelines over and over again. If you have exhausted these ideas and they aren't working for you, you may want to consider redesigning or modifying your overall *personal brand.*

Designing a personal brand

Let's talk for a minute about a self-developing technique called personal branding and about how it can impact our social life and friendships.

It might sound weird at first, but have you ever thought of yourself as a brand before?

First off, what is a brand? Think of your favorite company and about what they produce, whether it is a product or service. Your favorite brand can be anything. It might represent food, clothing, athletic gear, cars, or anything else.

Name your favorite brand. What is it called?

Example: My favorite brand is Aster-Blu Apparel Company.

____

____

Think about the image of your favorite brand. What do you see?

Example: I see good quality merchandise, comfortable, and fashionable.

____

____

Think about the emotions that this brand gives to you. What do you feel?

Example: This brand makes me feel confident and relaxed.

____

____

Why is this your favorite brand?

Example: I feel that this brand fits my personality.

____

____

As weird as it may sound, just like your favorite company brand, everyone in their own way has a living, breathing, moving, human brand. Your brand is a combination of how other people see you and of what they feel when around you. It's what creates the emotions, perceptions and the experiences that people have simply from you being yourself.

Try this experiment: Think of someone you know. Close your eyes and say their name. What do you see? What is their image like? How does the thought of that person make you feel? Pay attention to the sensations and experience that the person gives to you.

Think of someone you know well. What is their name?

____

What do you see when you imagine this person? What is their image like?

____

____

How does the thought of this person make you feel?

____

____

What you see and feel is that person's personal brand! You have created an impression of that person in your mind subconsciously. Just like them, you have your own brand, which exists in the minds of other people in the same way. And this brand of yours ties directly into the friendships that you create.

Brands are much more than a visual product. Brands give an entire sensational experience.

People think of company brands with having specific attributes. Human brands are no different. These are a few of those attributes:

Attributes of a brand

- Quality: When people think of brands, they automatically connect them to their quality, whether the brand is good, bad, innovative and authentic, etc.
- Relevance: People measure a brand's relevance to their own values and to what they deem to be important.
- Distinguishing: A distinguishing brand stands out as something that people can believe in and something they can place their confidence in.
- Consistency: A good brand can be trusted to give a consistent experience every time. People gain loyalty to brands that they can rely on.

In the social world, people are going to think of you (and your brand) by using these same attributes. They will think about your quality of person. They will actually think of you using adjectives such as good, bad, strange, funny, unique, quiet, etc. They will compare your relevance to what they find to be important. They will determine if you share the same interests, beliefs, values, hobbies, and activities as they do. And lastly, they will watch to see if you are consistently someone they want to spend their time with.

What kind of brand do you want to portray to people?

Describe the personal brand that you want have. When someone closes their eyes to think of you, what do you want them to experience?

Example: I want my brand to be positive. When people think of me, I want them to envision someone happy, full of life, and I want them to feel motivated.

____

____

____

What words should describe the *quality* of your personal brand.

Example: My brand should be seen as realistic, exciting, sincere, and easy going.

____

____

____

What are some topics your brand is relevant to? What are your interests?

Example: My brand is artistic and creative. Anything that has to do with modern or abstract art relates to me because that's what I find most interesting.

____

____

____

What makes you distinguishing? Why can people believe in you?

Example: I keep promises. I hold to my word. People learn that when they confide in me, I'm there for them.

____

____

____

Just as people can find a favorite brand in a company, people will see your personal brand and will decide whether or not to become your friend based on the experiences that you give to them. When we become the brand that we want to be, we find the friends that we want to have.

Branding isn't everything.

Personal branding helps us design and modify the person we want to be so that we can better reach our objectives in a social environment. It's a way of saying, "I can be who I want to be, and I can help people see that person within me." But personal branding is not everything. We also need to identify genuine friends from among the crowd—friends that will last forever.

Identifying Friends

Solid friendships are like pillars of support that we can rely on within a social environment. When we have good friends they influence our whole life, even when we find ourselves alone. That inner feeling of certainty, of knowing that somewhere out there is someone who cares, is a feeling that doesn't have a price.

The best friend of someone with scars or disfigurement is a friend unusually special. These are friends who have an eye for what makes the whole value of a person, and they have the heart for what's really important in a relationship.

The following pages contain characteristics that help identify a genuine friend. For those who have scars or a disfigurement, it is suggested that you compare your current friends to these attributes, and as new friends are made, use these attributes as a template for determining how genuine they really are.

Friends are Comfortable

A genuine friend is going to feel comfortable around you. This means they feel undisturbed and free. Being comfortable with you means your presence and personality awaken them to a sense of happiness. They like you, and they enjoy being around you. A genuine friend is not going to feel alienated or uneasy by the fact that you have an abnormal appearance. They know that your scars, disfigurement and overall image are part of who you are; they recognize that and have accepted them just as they have accepted you.

How have you determined that a friend is comfortable with you?

____

____

____

____

Friends are Trusting

One way to determine a high level of friendship is by measuring the amount of trust within the relationship. Trusting a friend means each of you can rely on the integrity of the other. You can share personal information with them in confidence, including secret thoughts and emotions revolving around your scars, traumas, or anything else. You can share private information without battling resistance and with a surety that your trust will not be betrayed.

How have you determined that you can trust your friends?

____

____

____

Friends have Loyalty

A genuine friend is a loyal friend, and by being loyal these friends hold true to their commitments, obligations, and oaths. As a friend, they have agreed to stand by you, to stand up for you, and to watch for anything that could bring you harm. When their loyalty is tested, a genuinely loyal friend never wavers. When opposition arises, whether it be in the form of a bully, a personal struggle, or an unexpected adversity, this friend remains by your side until whatever it is that's bothering you is over and gone.

How have you determined that your friends are loyal to you?

____

____

____

Friends Listen

Genuine friends can be identified by their active listening skills. A genuine friend doesn't do all of the talking. They have valid interest in you and in your interests. Hearing you express yourself brings them gratification. They take what you say seriously, and your opinions have major influence on them.

How have you determined that your friend is a good listener?

____

____

____

Friends aren't limited by Touch

Touching is not crucial, but friends should be able to have physical contact without feeling awkward about it. Where a lot of people might feel uncomfortable touching someone with scars or a disfigurement, a genuine friend does not. They know to respect your limits, values, and principles. Touching does not have to be romantic or sensual. It can be as casual as a handshake or a hug, but at any level, touching is an action that communicates familiarity, closeness, intimacy and bond. Certain barriers don't exist in friendship, and the tactile senses are a way to show it.

How have you determined that touch is not a barrier in your friendships?

____

____

____

Friends are Sensitive

When you're not feeling at your best, a genuine friend knows it. They can sense your ups and downs almost as well as you can. They also know if and when you have been offended because usually they will take offense along with you. They are aware and responsive to your feelings because by emotional connection, their own feelings are impacted by them. A genuine and sensitive friend is also a supportive friend who knows that discussing your scars or disfigurement might be a delicate topic that you'd rather avoid talking about; nonetheless, this friend is willing to talk at any time.

How have you determined that your friend is sensitive?

____

____

____

Friends are Protecting

When identifying a genuine friend, you're not necessarily looking for a bodyguard, per se, but you do want someone who will go to bat for you and defend you from harm if necessary. This attribute, just like the rest of them is a reciprocal one. Friendships are mutual, and that means you behave like a friend for them. Just as you don't want to see your friend get hurt or feel depressed, they shouldn't want to see you depressed. A genuine friend protects you from feeling sad and upset to their best ability. They work to keep your spirits up and to keep you focused on what's good.

How have you determined that your friend protects you?

____

____

____

Friends are Motivating

Finally, a genuine friend is also your best motivator. They want you to succeed more than anything, and they promise to be there until you champion your goals. A motivating friend uses words, creative ideas, clever thoughts, and their own ingenuity as resources to help you along. They ask questions and spark new concepts that fill you with inspirational energy. You know a genuine friend when they refuse to do anything that would hold you back or slow you down. When they see that you are in a slump, they are there to quickly pick you up and carry you onward.

How have you determined that your friend motivates you?

____

____

____

At the same time that we learn to identify a genuine friend, it's equally important to be one in return. Even though our friends may not have scars or a disfigurement like we do, every one of these characteristics should describe our own behavior. The better of a friend we are to them, the better our friends will be to us.

Conclusion

Friends are whom we cling to for support in a social environment. We all need them.

We are all in search for genuine friendships, the ones that last forever. There are things we can do to create them and maintain them. This includes following the basic pattern of sociability that exists for all people as well as designing and managing our personal brand.

Because we want friends that will endure and thrive with us, we must learn to recognize who a true friend is by their distinguishing qualities and the things they do. We must also learn to be a genuine friend in return.

LIFE AT SCHOOL

School can be a great dichotomy, a make or break environment, to the convincing of one that they are either great and that the future is bright, or that the world is cruel and that almost nothing is worth striving for.

What will school be for you?

Summary

There is no environment quite like school. With hordes of obstacles to be faced, you're entrenched in an education system encountering ultimatums that will uncompromisingly define you as a person. If you want to, you can gain a clear idea about who you really are on the inside. Opportunities are given to you to explore your ambitions, discover your true weaknesses, and fortify your skills.

When you look exceptionally different, school can be scary and overwhelming. More than a few have compared it to a place of incarceration, describing the experience in the same fashion as would a prisoner trapped in jail. But should this be any surprise to us? When we stop and examine what goes on, it's obvious as to why.

Brandon, a client from Rare Cases once said,

"There is nothing good to say about me attending school. Imagine being the student that everyone picks on and for reasons that you cannot control. You try to mind your own business, but you can hear people talking about you, laughing at your scars, and mocking you from all directions. I never know what's going to happen next. Classmates pick on me and criticize me all the time because of how I look. That's something that I cannot change. Trust me; I would if I could. Most days I sit alone and wander the halls by myself. I know my teachers care about me, but they don't know how to help. Concentrating on schoolwork and homework is pretty much impossible. Nothing motivates me. Even my parents know that by now. Besides, if no one wants to include me or befriend me at school because of how I look, it's a sign that the world won't do much better once it's over."

Brandon's experience is a standard model of what students with visible differences often go through because school and prison can have many similarities when you have a visible difference. The amount of bullies, the heightened anxiety, a severe lack of motivation, and loneliness are only some of the common aspects. The bright side, however, is that school is *not* a prison. No matter how much it might seem like it is, literally, it is not. Each of us can make a difference at school in ways that are plainly impossible in a prison environment. We can improve the educational experience; we just have to learn how.

The following pages contain suggestions for improving your life at school. But before we dive into that, let me first tell you a story of my own.

Brady's Story

It was the beginning of my eighth grade year. My family had spent the whole summer moving into a new home. This was the fourth house we'd live in since I started the fifth grade. One house a year average was getting to be way too much change for me! Each neighborhood and school came with an array of new challenges for me to face. It seemed that as soon as I was able to adjust to one place and to a new group of people, it was time to pack up and start over again. The circumstances that I alone had to deal with were terrible. Anyone who moves around that much knows that when you're young, adjusting can be hard. Well, the "hard" part multiplies drastically when you are someone facially disfigured like me.

Graduation wouldn't come fast enough! The accumulated troubles of school by then had me exhausted. What would the new year bring? The same pattern as always—guaranteed. I was sure I could count on the bullies, the strange looks, discrimination, and rejections to come at me, but would there be at least one kid who would see past my looks and want to be my friend? I had serious doubts, and I had my reasons for doubting it.

My projections were disastrously accurate. That new school had more unfriendly students than any other I had previously attended. For the first couple of weeks, to keep my sanity I did nothing but sit alone, roam the halls by myself, and gaze at the clock until the bell rang. You know things are going poorly when your objective every day is to avoid people. The year had just started and I had already been given the new kid treatment with the additional labels of "the new handicapped kid," "scar face," and "the freak." Those titles along with my monotonous routine continued until the day that I finally snapped.

It was the third Friday of the school year. I sat and waited on a curbside for the sight of my mother's approaching car. "Where is she?" I stammered. "I need to get out of here! I swear this time I'm never coming back." As I sat and stared off into the distance, a bus full of kids rolled up and parked directly in front of me, completely blocking my view. I looked up into the windows and observed the kids as they laughed and threw papers at each other. Their idea of school is so different from mine, I thought. Their lives seem so foreign. It's as if they're from a whole different planet as me.

Sitting in the very back seat of the bus was a tall lanky kid, who, for some reason had spotted me. "Hey, scar face!" he yelled, his long, floppy arm dangling out the window towards me. "Everyone, look at this loser! I think half his face blew up or something!"

At that moment a handful of other kids crowded around the windows to see what the fuss was about. In unison, they began mocking and howling at me like I was some kind of joke. "That's gross! What a weirdo! Hey, poser, your face looks like raw hamburger meat!" A couple of them were pulling at the skin on their own faces to exaggerate the method of ridicule.

I was emotionally spent. All of this was too much for me to take, but I stayed in the path of their fire until the bus shook and rolled away. It was bad. It was very bad. The only thing they could have done worse at that moment would have been to scurry off the bus and beat my head into the sidewalk.

In less than a minute more, I saw my mom's car making its way over. What a relief! When she stopped, I quickly opened the passenger door and climbed into the front seat.

"How was school?" Mother asked.

I was silent.

She put her hand on my shoulder. "Is everything all right, son?

From the tone of her voice I knew she had already read right through me. Not only did she know I had a bad day, she was so in tune with everything that she knew what it was all about.

"Kids are making fun of your scars again, aren't they, honey."

"I'm not going back there, Mom. I can't! Please don't make me go back there. It's not going to stop, and I can't do this again. Why did we have to move? I was happier at the last school. At least I was starting to make some friends."

She held my hand and gave it a gentle squeeze. "You're really done aren't you, sweetie."

"I'm done, Mom. I'm really, really done!"

"Well... I'm done with it all, too."

She didn't need any more convincing. My mom wanted the very best for me that she could give, so instead of heading home, she took a detour and immediately drove across town to the school district office, determined to have a meeting with the superintendent of education. She was going to give them her piece.

At first I was surprised to see how fast she was addressing the issue. She didn't waste any time at all. I didn't even have to elaborate on my day's experience or tell her about the kids on the bus. Of course, it wouldn't be the first time we'd talk about that sort of problem. We had already discussed leaving that school before. Mom was going to take me out for sure now, but not without raising some hell first.

We arrived at the district office seconds before they closed, but that didn't matter. Mom insisted that we have a minute with the man in charge. The superintendent was cordial and awake to the fact that we had something important to address. Mom did all of the talking, and I rolled with it. She knew my situation well enough to say what had to be said. It was obvious she was there on a mission—to pull me out of my current school and obtain permission to attend my previous school, far outside the boundaries of where we lived. Doing so would require the man's signature. Within minutes, she had what she needed. The man learned very quickly that no one gets in the way of Mom! But for everything to be concrete, subsequent meetings would have to be held with the vice principle of each school. We'd have to obtain their signatures as well. She did.

The following school day I was enrolled in the school of my choice. Mom was my hero! She made it happen. Without her involvement, I would have been continuously victimized and unwillingly incarcerated in that school-like prison. But that wasn't going to happen. Instead, I was going to be studying alongside familiar faces with fewer worries on my mind. Thanks to Mom's support and bold decision-making, I would eventually graduate from the school that offered me enough good memories to last a lifetime.

What can be learned from this story?

What were some of Brady's main worries about attending a new school?

____

____

____

____

What experiences did he describe that made school similar to a prison?

____

____

____

____

What was good about the communication that Brady had with his mother?

____

____

____

____

What attributes did his mother have that made a big difference in his educational life?

____

____

____

____

Education and Intervention

Every school has students living with a visible difference and who are likely to encounter prejudice and social stigmas on a daily basis. Although several of them will manage to succeed on their own, many deal with psychological setbacks that not only impact their emotional well-being, but will also result in less driven academic performance and underachievement.

With the right kind of intervention, the learning experience for these students can be more rewarding. They can learn to excel academically and socially regardless of what they look like.

Rejection and Discrimination at School

Rejected and discriminated. These are the terms most often used by students with visible differences when describing the challenges they face at school.

Why are they rejected and discriminated?

Answer: These students are discriminated for how they look. They're rejected for how they don't fit the status quo defined by society and their peers and for how their presence make others feel.

What are they rejected from?

Answer: Students with visible differences are often rejected from social groups and activities that occur both inside and outside of the classroom. It has also been found that because they look different, they are frequently rejected opportunities to express themselves credibility when participating in class discussions and projects.

Have you ever experienced rejection or discrimination at school because of the way you look? If so, in what ways have you been rejected or discriminated against?

____

____

____

____

Rejection and discrimination at school can be remedied and overcome!

Rejection and discrimination at school can be much less of a problem than it is for you now. Don't ever feel like you're stuck in the situation that you're currently in. A major lesson that can be learned from Brady's story is that a learning environment can be strategically changed and improved. The example was given when Brady and his mother met with the school superintendent to find the best learning environment possible for him. Several ideas had already been pursued before changing schools became a necessary solution. Obviously, changing schools is not going to be an option for everyone, but improving any current learning environment most definitely is!

The school can help

The following ideas are given for schools to improve the learning environment and provide a remedy for rejection and discrimination. In particular, these are things that the school can do on behalf of a student with a visible difference.

- Collaborate. School administrators can collaborate ideas from target groups to improve the learning environment and reduce stress for someone with a visible difference. Target groups include parents, teachers, school counselors, administrators, and in many cases fellow students. Many solutions are found when these groups come together to brainstorm ideas.

- Survey. Schools can perform internal research to acquire valuable feedback from students through the use of surveys. A school can measure and identify discrimination factors and pinpoint reasons for rejection. Surveys give students a chance to express their experiences, opinions, and ideas anonymously to their teachers. The information the students voluntarily give can help school officials direct change wherever necessary.

- Discuss. Faculty can hold meetings and workshops to discuss present discriminating conditions observed towards a particular group or student. Together they can set goals and make plans to generate change wherever needed. They can follow up and report as a group to measure progress.

- Provide resources. Schools are the perfect place to provide students with a visible difference, the right resources and learning materials they need. This self-guided course by Rare Cases titled *Life with Scars,* for example, can be made available to students from the school library or media center. Schools should allow students with visible differences time to work through these kinds of materials.

- Mentoring. School counselors can suggest to students with a visible difference that they work with a professional mentor. A mentor is someone who can relate firsthand to the student's experiences. Mentors are individuals who provide valuable feedback, expert advice and training in ways that a teacher, school counselor and parent generally cannot.

- Motivate. Schools can hire motivational speakers to help educate the entire student body on the topics of visible differences and the influence of prejudiced behavior. Speakers can come into the classroom or an assembly to inspire the students, motivate them, and encourage necessary changes of behavior.

If you feel that any of these ideas would help improve your current learning environment, you're encouraged to bring this list of ideas to your school administrators so that change can begin immediately. By visiting with the school board and discussing these things with them, you might also learn from them about any additional options that are already available to you.

Which of these ideas would you like to see implemented at your school? List all that could apply.

____

____

____

____

Is there anything else that you plan to discuss with your school administrators?

____

____

____

____

Things a Parent Can Do

If you are the parent of a student who is encompassed by the obstacles at school because of a visible difference, there are many things that you can do to assist them. Of course you, more than anyone, have their well-being and educative potential in mind. The following ideas are given to point you in the right direction.

- Listen to your student. The first and foremost thing a parent or guardian can do to help their student is listen to their emotions, thoughts, and pleas even if you are unable to grant them their every want or request. By never failing to listen, you are communicating that their experiences and desires matter.

- Give suggestions. Many times a parent perceives that they don't know enough or understand enough to give a valuable suggestion. Others have already suggested so many ideas that they are exhausted by their results not panning out the way they had imagined. Keep brainstorming. Keep suggesting. If anything, your ideas still provide the necessary encouragement that your student needs to receive from you.

- Be very patient. Be very patient not only with the obstacles of school itself, but also be patient with yourself and with your student's progress. Know that these things take time to improve.

- Get involved. You are your student's advocate. You are their number one supporter, their promoter, and their defender. Although you cannot save them from all of their challenges, by being involved they see that you care about them. Getting involved in their school life includes talking to school officials whenever necessary, being willing to advocate on your student's behalf to administrators, and by seeking answers to their challenges the way a true advocate should.

- Make bold decisions. As a parent you have the power to select the environment where your student will learn. Don't underestimate that role. You hold executive power and have supervisory authority to your student's well-being. You are a legislator in that you can take part in setting rules and guidelines that the school will support. You are also a judge. Open your ears and open your eyes. You can discern levels of hostility within a school and can determine if the place is right for your student to attend. You have the ability to change the environment at any time. If the setting isn't right, you have the power to pull them out and relocate. Because you know your student, a bold decision can also mean it's right for them to stay and stick it out.

If you are a parent or guardian, what things can you do to improve your student's life at school?

If you are a student, what things should your parent or guardian do?

____

____

____

____

____

____

Discuss together as parent/guardian and student any changes that can be made together to improve life at school. List those changes here.

____

____

____

____

____

Things the Student Can Do

As a student, you are the chieftain standing at the helm of your own future. It's obvious that your academic situation is a highly unique one. You're probably the only, or one of few students at your school who have an abnormal appearance, and as such you automatically stand out from the rest. Because you're different, you might view school as a major dilemma. The good news is there are things within your grasp that you can do for your own benefit and intellectual growth.

- Believe in yourself. I know it sounds cliché and perhaps mundane, but this is something you have to do. Believe that within you is a potential that you do not yet comprehend, no matter what condition you're in. In reality, none of us know what we are capable of, and none of us know how much we can overcome until opportunities arise for us to be tested. People can tell you differently every day—that you can't overcome—and school is the number one place where they will do so. People can put you down and say you're worthless. They can slander and defame you for how you look, but the only person who decides if what they say is true or not is you! Words can degrade, but humiliation is a reaction we make by choice. Every time we decide to press on through the fiery darts of our perpetrators, we take one step closer to our potential. Along the way, we refine ourselves. We become stronger when we believe in our untapped potential. After great tribulation is even greater reward. Believe that. Train yourself to endure all things. Believe in yourself and you'll come out of school a champion.

- Welcome criticism. If you haven't learned by now that attitude is everything, here it is in black and white: ATTITUDE IS EVERYTHING!! Trying to avoid criticism at school is like running naked through a rainforest during a storm and trying to stay dry. Good luck with that. You will get wet. Everyone, even the most attractive individuals get criticized at school. As people with abnormal appearances, handling criticism for us should become second nature. We're not going to succeed at making it stop, so instead, we're going to do the opposite and welcome criticism as it is dished out to us.

Welcoming criticism does not mean accepting and believing what people say and think about us. It doesn't mean supporting or endorsing their opinions. When we welcome criticism we merely allow it to happen. We allow ourselves to be different. End the fight with peace of mind. Any of us can clinch our fists, grit our teeth, cry, or stomp our feet. We can yell all we want, but if we do, criticism will continue to pester us until the day's end. On the other hand, if we decide not to do those things and instead carry on our merry way, things will improve for us. The decision is up to you.

When people criticize they measure one's quality; they look for faults and defects. So, go ahead and let people criticize you! What are they going to find that you don't already know about? Sure, they'll add an ignorant and biased judgment against you, one that probably has been repeated over a thousand times, but in the grand scheme of things, who cares what they think? The reality is that whatever they find odd or eccentric about you and criticize you for is a confession that they are severely precarious and apprehensive. One thing is for certain—they obviously need more help than you!

- Develop new skills. Since we're talking about school, clearly we need to address the importance of getting educated. School was established for us to expand our knowledge base while we're there. We aren't in school solely to gain a social life. By improving and widening our skills, a lot of other things are likely to improve, too, including how we get along with others. As a person becomes talented in any topic, their talents always have a way of outshining the way they look. People become focused on what they can do well.

  It's extremely important that we become smarter, more skilled, and more diverse for our own sake. Certainly opportunities and the quality of life increases substantially when we are educated. There are more things to do, more places to go, and more activities to enjoy when we engage in continuous learning. Whether it’s a foreign language we learn, or picking up a new trade, mastering a subject at school, growing a sense of entrepreneurship, or anything else, developing new skills broadens our horizons and make us more eclectic individually.

- Place your aim high. What are your goals for your education? Where do you want your education to take you? What do you aspire to be and what do you want to do once your schooling is complete? Will your schooling ever be complete? These are big questions that beg for big answers. Your education will take you as far as you want it to, depending on how you manage it. Whatever you do, don't be the person that calls it quits for the wrong reasons.

No matter how bad your situation gets at school, you have to learn to see above and beyond what's happening right now around you. You have to keep your vision into the future and your aim set high.

Our Physical and Emotional Limits

Let's talk about the specific things that keep us limited. Certain activities, like athletics or dance might be physically impossible for you to participate in if your body is not built for it. Other activities might be emotionally impossible to do. Whether you have physical limitations or emotional ones, it's important to recognize specifically what they are and what prevents you from enjoying full participation at school. When you know what your limits are you can gain a better idea about how you are to go beyond them.

Physical Limitations

Physical limitations vary by degree and can be classified as impairments, disabilities, or handicaps. Read the following definitions of each and then decide if any or all apply to you.

Impairment: You have impairment when your scar or disfigurement has caused a loss or abnormality of an anatomical, psychological, or physiological structure or function. This means that something considered a normal bodily structure or function has been lost or permanently changed. Most all scars and disfigurements automatically fall under this category.

Disability: Scars and disfigurements become a disability when they restrict or prevent you from having the ability to perform an activity in a range considered to be normal.

Handicap: The keyword with handicap is "disadvantage." You have a handicap if your scars or disfigurement limit you from fulfilling a role because of an anatomical, psychological, or physiological disadvantage. Examples would be the inability to walk, use both arms, or speak.

Are there any activities at school that you would like to participate in, but you feel that you are *physically* limited and unable to do so? What activities are they?

____

____

____

____

Physical limitations often cannot be fixed entirely; however, alternative solutions can be found. One who is unable to play sports or dance, for example, can learn to enjoy different activities within the scope of their physical abilities.

Don't get hung up on the things that you cannot do. Instead, remain focused on the things that you can do. Magnify those abilities and search for new, additional skills to have.

What alternative activities can you participate in, or what is an unlearned skill that you can develop in place of the activities you cannot do?

____

____

____

____

Emotional Limitations

Most students who are struggling with scars or a disfigurement at school are wrestling with emotional limitations. They're either dealing with social pressure, prolonged depression, or a lack of confidence, and because of these struggles they tend to isolate themselves.

Overcoming Self-imposed Isolation

Self-imposed isolation occurs when we separate ourselves from other people on a regular basis. This usually happens with feelings of inadequacy and extreme sensitivity to the negative evaluation they receive from other people. The following guidelines can help in overcoming self-imposed isolation:

Identify what you're going through. If you are suffering with self-imposed isolation, wake up to the habit of avoiding people. Identify exactly when and why you are avoiding opportunities to be social. Note the feelings that are aroused when you isolate yourself from people. Do you feel anxious, fearful, unqualified, unappealing, lonely, or socially inept?

When and why do you avoid the opportunity to be social?

____

____

____

____

What feelings do you have when you isolate yourself?

____

____

____

____

Be productive. Our alone time is important, and what we do with the alone time is even more important. When you are alone do you spend time feeling sorry for yourself, or do you do productive things?

Find at least one activity that you would regularly enjoy doing alone, but that could potentially involve additional people. This activity can be in or out of school. It can be as simple as reading a book and then talking about the story or topic that you've read with someone else. It can be watching your favorite television show and then watching the show with someone else. Even a casual walk to the park can be shared with another person.

What activity do you do alone that could potentially involve more people?

____

____

____

____

Start a partnership. You might feel alone, but you are not the only one feeling isolated. Someone else is experiencing the same kind of isolation not very far away. Find that person and begin a partnership together. If it doesn't work out, search for someone else who you can begin to share time with.

Work with a mentor who understands your struggles and who has already lived through what you are grieving. Visit with your mentor on a regularly scheduled basis, even when you do not want to. To overcome self-imposed isolation we need regular contact with someone. Whether our partnerships are with a classmate, a family member, teacher, a support group, or a professional, by having one-on-one time with someone regularly, we gradually end the pattern of isolation.

Lifestyle Alteration and Re-Entry Programs

Many of us are survivors of events or experiences that have altered our lives forever. Before they happened we were someone. We had the same name and the same family as we do now. We came from the same place and might carry the same memories, but since then our person and way of life might have changed. How can we be expected to act the same and to be the same as we were before? Are we to carry on as if the trauma never happened? Are we to keep the same attitude and personality as we had before? With so much being different about us now, it is highly unlikely that our lifestyle will stay the same as it was before.

School is one of the places where a re-entry program may be necessary for you to experience successful adaptation. Most students who have experienced a lifestyle-altering event need some kind of re-entry program. At school we're surrounded by people who don't understand what we've been through, and who naturally want us to return as the same person we were before we left. Of course, having this expectation isn't even rational, but they simply don't understand. We're different now. We've changed. Now it's time for everyone to adapt to those changes.

A re-entry program refers to the time of transition that students make back to school after they have experienced something traumatic. Re-entry programs are also available for any students who will be attending a school for the first time. In the program the student and their family work with professionals who facilitate a smooth transition by working as a mediator between them and the school.

Deciding on a re-entry program for yourself or for your student can be overwhelming if you don't have any guidance. Where do you start looking? Who is qualified to assist with re-entry, and how will they make the transition a smooth process? To find the best program available, look for one that will include at least the following steps. Knowing these things will happen should take most of the worry away as you can be certain that the process is happening the right way.

The following procedure should be carried out on your behalf to facilitate a smooth and rewarding re-entry experience by the professional or group that you choose:

- The re-entry professionals will sit with the student and their family prior to re-entry. They should become familiarized with the traumatic story and address any initial concerns that anyone in the family may have about returning to school.

- Re-entry professionals will coordinate assignments with the school and will hold meetings with faculty prior to the student's re-entry. These meetings allow key stakeholders the chance to become familiarized with the student's story and to become acquainted with the student well before their arrival to school.

- Re-entry professionals work with the school and arrange for speakers and educators who will train and prepare the student body for the student's return. This will be done without revealing any intimate or confidential information. The messages will be designed and delivered to raise awareness to the challenges of living with visible differences and the messengers involved will respect the privacy and confidentiality of the student in question. At the same time they will communicate to the student body the urgency of having respect and the ability to tolerate the visible differences of one another.

- A re-entry program will include scheduled follow up appointments with the student and their family. They will revisit the original challenges and will measure the progress that has been made over time. New goals and plans will be set in motion that further enhances the student's long-term experience at school.

Is there anything else you would expect or hope to receive from a re-entry program? List those things here and then discuss them with the program director.

____

____

____

____

____

Conclusion

In every school there are students with a visible difference. Most of these students undergo severe challenges within their educational environment. Many describe school as a prison, and the amount of discrimination and rejection surrounding them is abnormally high. The obstacles they face can be overcome, but it requires team effort from themselves, their parents, and school faculty by coming together with common goals and fulfilling separate responsibilities. There are things the school can do to help the student. There are things the parent can do, and there are things the students can do to help themselves.

Scars and disfigurement bring physical and emotional limitations. Depending on how limited the student is tells a lot about what kinds of activities they can participate in and fully enjoy. If certain skills or activities cannot be performed, alternative ones can be found. Any student can acquire enough skills to be successful. Self-imposed isolation is a common example of an emotional limitation brought on by a number of reasons. Students can overcome self-imposed isolation by following a series of steps.

For students who have been through a life-altering experience from trauma, an effective re-entry program may be necessary when transitioning back into school or when entering a new school for the first time. Re-entry programs are designed to make the transition a smooth one.

The overall lesson that we can learn from this section is that so much of our educational experience can be managed. We can each make school a positive experience by learning the role we play and by working together.

LIFE AT WORK

At work we strive for secure opportunities, custody over our accomplishments, and guaranteed insurance that our contributing efforts are for a greater good. Sometimes these things are achieved with little exertion; other times we have to fight for them.

Summary

If you don't have an automatic source of financial income to sustain you with the necessities of life, then like me you have to rely on work and understand that what abounds in great plenty are the challenges of the workplace. It would be wonderful if people with visible differences were treated fairly at work, free of discrimination and prejudice, but evidently this has never been the case. Everywhere, in every job market the majority of individuals with a visible difference are seen as being prone to fail job interviews, less likely to be promoted, and more apt to make customers and co-workers feel uncomfortable with them around.

In a perfect world, each of us would be judged professionally based on our merits alone and not by what we look like. We'd be measured according to the results of our efforts and not by our physical imperfections. But look around; we aren't in a perfect world, are we? No. In the real world we're often judged prematurely and discriminated against because of our appearance.

Men and women of great enlightenment have preached doctrines of anti-discrimination many times before. Granted them, it is a very attractive message and one that strikes a chord with the soul. "The world would be a better place if people were judged strictly by the content of their character and not by what they look like." If only everyone practiced this heavenly message many of our problems would cease to exist. But powerful as it may be, this message that has been continuously belted from the rooftops is yet to be implemented by society as a whole.

If you are a current job seeker, an employee, or an employer of any kind, this lesson is for you because everyone plays a valuable role in making life at work a constructive experience. This section outlines common work topics and provides answers to frequent questions that arise surrounding the workplace for anyone with scars or disfigurement that is either preparing or working to maintain a job.

A Word to Employers and Interviewers

Workplace discrimination is a moral and ethical crime and in most circumstances is a legal crime as well. Historically, employment discrimination and merit resolution have seen unfavorable disproportion regarding offerings extended to individuals with visible differences. As a key stakeholder in the success or failure of these job candidates, the importance of your judgment as

an employer or interviewer in being fair and unbiased is of monumental significance. As you commence your next hiring process, remember to judge according to the quality and content of your candidate's character. Base your decision on the skills and abilities that they offer instead of basing a decision merely on what the candidate looks like.

Applications and Resumes

Many individuals wonder if they should explain on an application or resume that they have a scar or disfigurement. Is this a necessary step? The answer is very simple. No, it isn't necessary, and giving the employer that information about you prior to an interview gives them an excuse to deny you an equal opportunity. Think about this for a second. Isn't it hard to communicate your personality and charisma without meeting someone directly? An employer deserves the chance to meet you, and you deserve the chance to show them who you are, face to face or over the phone, before their hiring decision is made.

Many employers are using social media to get an inside scoop to the personal life of their job candidates. This happens regularly before and after interviews are taking place. In some places it has become a standard practice for companies to require a picture portrait to be affixed to an applicant's resume. Isn't it obvious that this could be detrimental to anyone with a visible difference looking for a job? Such actions incontestably cause workforce discrimination. Whether or not this or a similar practice is happening where you live, be mindful that any pictures and information not related to work on social media sites are easily accessible to employers. They can and will be used inaudibly against you.

Your applications and resume should serve one united purpose: to promote you to the job that you're applying for. If any piece of information has a strong possibility to hinder your candidacy, simply don't include it unless required of you. If you are inclined to think the interviewer will judge you poorly because of a physical difference, save that topic for the interview when you can demonstrate to them how big or small of an issue it really is. Everything that is written down on an application and resume should stand as a testament that you are not only qualified for the job, but that you are also the best applicant on their list. Nothing less.

Interview Preparation

Common questions revolving around job interviews are:

- Should I mention my scars in a job interview?
- If the interviewer asks what happened to me, how should I answer?

A lot of anxiety goes into a job hunt. From the initial application process to the creation of a resume and up through the days leading to the interview, stress can be overwhelming for anyone. It isn't merely about how you feel or about how well you prepare that makes a difference in results, either. A large responsibility is on the interviewer to judge you fairly and in a way that is nondiscriminatory. Unfortunately, many interviewers will have a tendency to deny a job if the interviewing candidate has a significant visible difference about them.

Three Main Reasons why Scars and Disfigurement Impact an Interview

It shouldn't be surprising to learn that significantly visible scars and disfigurements can put an interviewer on edge by distracting or deterring them from an engaging conversation. Here are three major side effects of this, which you should be aware of before an interview ever takes place:

1. Interviewers can become distracted by a candidate's abnormal appearance and subsequently lose focus on the interview itself. After it's over, the interviewer may easily recall what the candidate looked like, but struggle to determine if the candidate really qualified for the job.

2. Interviewers can be concerned that since their candidate looks different, they might also be emotionally damaged. They perceive that self-esteem will be a roadblock making performing the tasks required of them difficult or impossible.

3. Interviewers get worried that co-workers and customers will react negatively to the new hire's abnormal appearance. They think they'll avoid unnecessary friction and the possibility of losing trust with customers if they don't bring someone who looks abnormal into the workplace.

Isn't it unlawful for employers to discriminate based on appearance?

Answer: It may be unlawful for an employer to discriminate, but studies show that appearance has significant influence on the success or failure of an interview. Workplace discrimination of this kind is common. Looks are only superficial, but people often judge based on what they see, especially when an interview is both the first time and a one-time opportunity to make an important decision.

What can I do to overcome workplace discrimination at an interview and land myself a job?

Answer: The top qualities that employers look for in job candidates are not superficial ones. By mastering the qualities that they look for, the likelihood of you being hired is dramatically improved. Don't underestimate your personality, charisma and interpersonal skills. They can outshine an abnormal appearance no matter what you look like. Prepare yourself in advance to leave a positive, memorable impact.

Top Qualities that Employers Look For in a Job Candidate

Directions: Review the top qualities that employers look for. After each one, explain how you can portray that quality in your own unique way.

Intelligence

First and foremost, know your stuff! Go into the interview with an intelligent mindset and with the ability to verbally articulate your knowledge base. An employer wants to see that you have done your research and that you knew something about the job you're interviewing for in advance to being there. They want to be sure that you are fully aware of what the job entails and that you know exactly what you're getting yourself into. Your intelligence is something that can be reflected in your resume, too. During the application stage, take time to communicate on your resume that you have an intelligent foundation, that you know what you're talking about, how you know what you know, and why.

How can you portray your intelligence to an employer?

____

____

____

____

Leadership Ability

Do you have what it takes to be a leader? If given the opportunity down the road, would you be both willing and capable to transition into a leadership role? An employer wants you to say yes. They want leadership ability because they want you to grow in the company. They want someone who is dedicated and committed to the job long term. They want a leader. Leaders are decision makers. Leaders are confident in themselves. Leaders have enough energy and drive to motivate a team. Are you a leader? Can you become a leader?

How can you portray that you have leadership ability?

____

____

____

____

Integrity

As someone with a high level of integrity you can discern between right and wrong, and you seek to do what is right under all circumstances. You're honest, sincere, and courageous to defend what is ethically and morally correct. An employer wants to hire someone with a strong sense of integrity because along with the job they are also offering a great deal of trust.

How can you portray to an employer that you have a high level of integrity?

____

____

____

____

Likeability

As would be assumed, someone who is exceptionally likable is someone who is friendly and has a positive attitude. But there is much more to being likable than being cheerful and wearing a smile. Likable people are engaged in their conversations. They are disciplined in their speech and mindful of their language. Because they're friendly they look for opportunities to compliment others. They bring a mellow tone and warmth to their relationships. Likable people are also amazing listeners who take care of information that's shared with them. They are patient and maintain calm composure, even in times of difficulty. They don't procrastinate. They seek opportunities to serve and they do tasks that are above and beyond what is asked of them.

How can you portray that you are a likable person?

____

____

____

____

Competence

When evaluating your competence for a job, ask yourself, “What makes me qualified?” Competence combines your intelligence, knowledge of the work involved, and any past experience you have in a related field. An employer knows that training you and getting you up to speed will be easier if you have some level of competence for that which you are being hired to do.

How can you portray a strong level of competence?

____

____

____

____

Inner Strength

Employers look to hire someone with inner strength because with it they can rely on you to be determined and steadfast when times get tough. By taking this course, you have exemplified that you are in tune with your inner strength. As someone with this quality, you have gained, or are gaining the ability to overcome life's adversities. Someone with a high level of inner strength has within them a sacred source of inner willpower, a sense of resilience. Employers should be mindful to the fact that interviews are pressure sensitive and often very stressful. If you can remain calm and relaxed in an interview, it is a sign that you have solid inner strength.

How can you portray that you have inner strength?

____

____

____

____

The Bonus Quality that Most Employers Look for:

Assertiveness

While on the job hunt each of us should portray the quality of assertiveness. This quality will directly correlate to how well we interview with a visible difference.

What does it mean to be assertive?

Assertive people know how and when to stand up for themselves. They are willing to defend their rights, beliefs, thoughts, and their feelings in a way that is honest and appropriate. Keep in mind that being assertive does not mean pushing your ideology onto other people. A big part of this quality is the ability to be respectful of the thoughts, feelings, and beliefs of other people. When you're assertive you are able to communicate your point of view in a way that is diplomatic and well mannered.

How does being assertive tie into having a visible difference when job searching?

When you're assertive you react constructively when a potential employer questions the impact that your appearance will have on your job performance, even if the topic never comes up in conversation. A lot of employers might wonder what happened to you. You don't have to spell it out on your resume, and you don't have walk into the interview declaring how your appearance never diminishes your quality of work, either. As a matter of fact, it is suggested that you don't do those things. But if during the interview you are asked what happened to make you look different, or you see that the interviewer is distracted by your appearance, then a pinnacle moment to be assertive has come.

What do you say to show that you're assertive?

Answer: Say two things.

1. First, say something that will shift the conversation to the topic of your abnormal appearance, *but do so without distancing yourself from the purpose of the interview.*

Here is an example:

"I am aware of the fact that many people in the workplace are curious about what my facial disfigurement is from. I'm not offended by their curiosity, and in fact, I would be curious as well."

2. Next, give a brief one line statement that tells them why you look different and then immediately explain how having this appearance has played a part in developing one or more of the top qualities that employers look for in a job candidate.

Here is an example that explains how disfigurement has promoted the quality of leadership:

"I look this way because of a genetic condition I have called cherubism. Having this condition has made me into a very confident individual. I know that diversity is a key element to a strong workforce, and what many people don't realize is that living with a disfigurement like mine not only makes one diverse, it also has a natural way of creating a strong sense of determination in a person. I know I look different, but because I do, I have had to be determined to live a successful life even when I look this way. I believe that I can apply my determination here, at this job, in a way that motivates other members of the team."

* This is an example of how being assertive can help turn an interviewer's curiosity around. Try connecting your scars or disfigurement to any one of the qualities that an employer looks for using an assertive explanation.

How can you demonstrate assertiveness in an interview and resolve an employer's curiosity?

1. First, say something that will shift the conversation to the topic of your abnormal appearance, *but do so without distancing yourself from the purpose of the interview.*

____

____

____

____

2. Next, give a brief one line statement that tells them why you look different and then immediately explain how having this appearance has played a part in developing one or more of the top qualities that employers look for in a job candidate.

____

____

____

____

Being the New Employee

Let's say you're a new hire. Congratulations on landing the job! Now you can start working and applying your talents and skills productively. As you go into this new venture, you might (as many of us have) find that your co-workers or customers have a hard time adjusting to you. You suspect that the reason they react strangely is because of the way you look. For help in recognizing different kinds of reactions that other people will make, see the section of this textbook called *Their Reactions* beginning on page 60. At work, co-workers and customers are some of the people most of us will see on a daily basis. Because of how often we are with them, some will eventually prod or show that they are curious to hear your story, and many individuals find that sharing their story can make working around them more enjoyable.

As said before, sharing your story with others should always be viewed as an opportunity. Work is no different.

Co-workers and customers don't always come with friendship. We've all had to put up with some that for some reason drive us absolutely crazy. Since you might be stuck with them, sharing your story can be an educative opportunity. Be assertive as you interact with these people, and most importantly, don't ever get offended by what a co-worker or customer says or thinks. You didn't get the job for them. You're there for yourself, and the people around you will have to either adjust to your appearance or move on. The choice is theirs.

How is sharing your story with co-workers and customers sometimes different than sharing it with other people?

____

____

____

____

What do you find to be the hardest part about being the new employee?

____

____

____

____

How have you responded when people at work become curious about you appearance?

____

____

____

____

Workplace Discrimination

If you feel that you have been subject to workplace discrimination or harassment, don't take the matter lightly. You are allotted the same legal protections as everyone else working there. You have the same rights as they do. Too many individuals feel that they can "remain tough" or "overlook the problem just fine," but these habits of avoiding confrontation have led to greater problems when the matter is not addressed.

There are two main reasons why *not* addressing workplace discrimination or harassment can be a problem for you:

1. You aren't protecting yourself from greater chances of harm.

2. You deny yourself certain rights.

A lot of us have a natural sense of resilience that has been crafted from overcoming trauma and hardship. When we get knocked down or insulted, we've learned to get right back up and brush it off like it never happened. Being resilient becomes a reflex, and when it does, pressing on happens automatically, no matter what challenge is against us. Because we are strong, we tell ourselves "we can deal with the adversity on our own." Resilience is a good thing to have, but it also comes with hazards. For example, resilience can get in your way from achieving greater things if you're allowing others to constantly put you down all the time without any consequence. If you are constantly tolerating workplace discrimination and harassment, your own sense of resilience is possibly getting in your way.

Laws Are in Place that Prohibit Discrimination and Harassment

Discrimination and harassment can take different forms. Broad-sweeping federal laws are in place to protect individuals in a wide variety of situations. If you are an employee who feels that you are being discriminated against or harassed by either your employer or a co-worker, know that there are several things you can do to protect yourself. Here is a short list of some of your options:

- Record in a log or agenda the events that are happening against you. Include the date, time, location, names of who was involved, and any witnesses who were present, and details of the situation where improper conduct or speech was occurring. Write down as much as you can, exactly as it happened, as soon afterwards as possible.

- Retain copies of any objects that were used in a way that was discriminatory or harassing towards you. Objects could include posted notes, pictures, posters, or letters that you happen to find. Keeping these items will help prove the validity of what happened once it is reported to the right people.

- Talk to your employer. Your direct supervisor or manager should be someone that you can go to for help. If you cannot talk to them, or if they are part of the problem, then contact the Human Resources Department or a person who is higher in command. When visiting with a representative of the company, make sure all of your conversations are documented for legal purposes.

  ** Be advised that falsely reporting discrimination or harassment to your employer could pose ramifications that would be unpleasant for you. Remember to always be honest.*

- For United States persons, contact the EEOC —the Equal Employment Opportunity Commission. If your employer doesn't take you seriously, or if there is no one in direct contact with you willing to help, you may find it necessary to get someone outside the organization involved. Contacting the EEOC is an option. The Equal Employment Opportunity Commission is an entity who oversees companies' compliance to federal anti-discrimination and anti-harassment laws. If you contact them, it is certain that they will be contacting your employer to get the matter resolved.

- Obtain a copy of the company policy where you work. Most companies have a written policy, posted and visible, for employees as a resource. When a company has an anti-discrimination and anti-harassment policy in place, they advertise and state that inappropriate behavior and conduct will not be tolerated. Ask your employer for a copy of the policy, or take a digital picture of the one that is posted. Keep the copy with you in your records.

- Review federal and state laws. Familiarize yourself with your rights. Laws are available to you and can be found at most libraries and on the Internet. The most applicable law in the United States outlining the rights and privileges for people with visible differences and disfigurement is the Americans with Disabilities Act, or ADA.

- Take time to review the ADA to see which sections of the law apply to your specific case. The following two basic points can be found:

    1. The ADA protects individuals who are regarded as having a substantially limiting impairment, even though they may not have such impairment. This provision protects individuals with severe facial disfigurement from being denied employment if and when an employer fears the reactions of their customers or co-workers.

    2. The ADA prohibits discrimination against certain disabled individuals and requires employers to make "reasonable accommodations" to allow access to buildings and functionality in the workplace.

** For more information on the Americans with Disabilities Act, to read frequently asked questions and answers, and to access the law in full text, visit www.ada.gov.*

- If necessary, work with an attorney. The results of workplace discrimination and harassment are always emotionally damaging. As the recipient of such conduct, the last thing you want to do is battle your way through the legal process of getting justice. Reading through piles and piles of laws in search for answers isn't something anyone should have to do when facing emotional trouble. An attorney is someone who can sort through the complexities of the legal process for you. The great thing about an attorney is that they are a third party looking in on the situation and are also your personal advocate. They will work to protect your rights while remaining calm and collective. Let them do the dirty job of reading through the laws and going to battle on your behalf. You stay focused on mending your emotions and getting back to work.

Why is it important to address workplace discrimination and harassment instead of always being resilient and allowing it to happen?

____

____

____

____

What is the name of the most applicable law in the United States that outlines the rights of someone with a visible impairment?

____

____

Why is it important to exercise your rights as an employee?

____

____

____

____

Working for Merit

Why do you work? What is your purpose for doing what you do professionally? Most of us have more than one reason for arriving to a job and for giving our best efforts day in and day out. Do you work because you are passionate about what you do? Are you trying to support yourself, or a family, too? Are you working only for the money? Is it about survival, paying bills, or are you working towards something bigger and better than what you already have? Do you work for the sake of staying busy, or is contributing to society and the community something that drives you there? Do you work purely for enjoyment? Think about this question. Any honest answer is a good one.

Why do you work? List your one or several reasons why.

____

____

____

____

The investment of our time at work cannot be replaced, repeated, or refunded, so for whatever reason you're working, it's important that you invest wisely in what you're doing.

For a lot of us, a huge chunk of our time will be spent at work. A major portion of our lives will be defined and valued by what we do there. If we allow it to, and if we plan for it to, work can provide us with sustainability and prosperity. Let's look ahead into the future. In five years you will be somewhere. In a decade you will be somewhere else. Where will you be? What kind of work will you be doing ten years from now, and how will your current work life help get you there?

Rhetorical questions:

- Is finding enjoyment in what you do enough of a reason to work?
- Is money enough reward to provide the life that you want?
- Will working to pay bills get you to the future that you envision for yourself?
- Does financially supporting yourself or a family define your life's work?
- Do you believe that you are capable of obtaining the professional lifestyle that you want to have?

** Your answers to these rhetorical questions are not right or wrong. These questions are here only to help you think about your direction.*

Here's a piece of advice. No matter what your goals are, or how far away from those goals you may be, go to work now in search of earning merit for a desired lifestyle.

What does it mean to work for merit?

Answer: When we work for merit, we strive to be worthy of a sufficient reward. When we merit something, we deserve to be awarded the worth of our accomplishments. Note that this does not always refer to a monetary reward. Ultimately, when we earn merit we take strides in the direction that we want to go and we become who we want to be.

Note:

- Earning merit does not mean receiving credit, pay, or increase. Merit is, however, being worthy and deserving of the credit, pay, or increase.
- If you merit something, it isn't automatically awarded to you, but you have, by all means, earned it.
- When you merit a lifestyle you don't necessarily have it, but you are indubitably qualified for it.

Earn merit for the lifestyle you want by becoming the person that you want to be professionally. Decide exactly what you want to achieve and what you want your life's work to be. Learn what it takes to get there, what it requires to be that person, and then gradually work in that direction. When you ask yourself where you want to be in five or ten years, follow up that question with another one—what will it take to get you there?

Identify the work that you want to do. It can be the same job that you have now, or it can be something else. Work can be defined by a title, a position in a company, a self-created project that you invent, or a type of service.

What is the work that you want to do in life?

____

____

____

____

Direction is happening to you no matter what. Time is passing by, and like everyone, you are headed in the direction of age. Unless death comes prematurely, you will eventually reach an age where you will not be able to work anymore. The vehicle carrying you through time is moving whether you like it or not. Figuratively speaking, are you in a train bound by the course of the tracks, or are you in a car? It's time to take control and steer yourself in the direction that you want to go. Ditch the train and grab the wheel. Decide on a direction professionally, and then go there.

What merits do you need in order to do the work you want to do? In other words, what would make you worthy or deserving of the work?

____

____

____

What is the life work that you want to be doing in five years?

____

____

____

____

What is the life work that you want to be doing in ten years?

____

____

____

____

How will your current life direct you to where you want to be?

____

____

____

____

What things will you do now to take control of your direction and go where you want to go?

____

____

____

____

Conclusion

Our lives at work will be successful if we have an understanding and comprehension of our capabilities and of our rights as professionals. The workplace can be full of discrimination and harassment, from the time of hiring and throughout a career. Although a lot of responsibility is on an employer to be fair and non-discriminatory, it is up to us to survive, thrive, and overcome these challenges.

There are a lot of reasons why we work, and everyone's reasoning is different. We all have different goals and ambitions. An important thing to realize is that your time spent at work is a huge investment. Time cannot be replaced, repeated, or refunded, and using it to take you in the direction that you want to go is critical.

Know what your life's work is and then prepare yourself to get it through merit. Become the professional that you want to be by doing the work that you want to do.

A life with scars might not be easy, but it is definitely worth it.

Summary

In this course, we've observed that virtually every part of life is affected by something outside our control—our scars. Clearly, a life with scars is not an easy one. You and I frequently deal with trials that most people won't ever have to. But as we've learned, behind the obstacles of life and within the turmoil of everyday adversity is the beauty of individual growth and room for emotional prosperity.

If we were to give in to our hardships, surrender our potential, and be overcome by the rage of life's forces, we'd wither away in defeat and never truly live the way we wanted to. We'd be outcasts, self-incriminators without a cause, or both. Our private life, public life, and social life would all languish. The vigor and vitality of living would be lost. And why? Because of the way we look or because of things we've been through. Those aren't reasons enough for me to suffer. I don't know about you, but I simply refuse to be defeated. Instead I choose the opposite—to succeed and beat the odds against me. I choose to thrive and to find fulfillment in what I do. Yes, I have scars. I am disfigured, but I refuse to be a victim to these things.

At Rare Cases we have a saying. "Rare cases are stories of people who overcome rare challenges." That saying describes the mindset that all of us should have. We have to come to the conclusion that suffering from our experiences is futile. Surviving them, championing them, overcoming them and thriving because of them is our calling. And friends, that's exactly what we're going to do. This life, the one you're living now is your story; it's your only story. It is a rare one, but a story that you can overcome and enjoy. If you're struggling at all, even in the slightest degree because of your scars or disfiguring appearance, keep going. Keep pushing on and keep applying these lessons to the conduct of your life. I promise, it will get better.

In this final section, I will show you through my own experience that successfully living with a visible difference might not be easy, but it is definitely worth it. Life can be as beautiful as we want it to be. It can be fulfilling; it can be edifying. This life with scars can even be romantic. I know it can because I've seen it in others, and it is for me.

What makes a life romantic?

A romantic life is the product of having certain qualities of living active. Those qualities are these: A life of purpose, a life with passion, a life with adventure, and a life of devotion. We find that if any one of these qualities is missing from the way we live, then life seems to lose its balance and its romantic touch rather quickly.

I will now break each of these qualities down and explain why each one is needed for a romantic life to be vibrant. As an anecdote, I'll share a few final lessons and will tell how these qualities have impacted my own life. Keep in mind that my story is not yours, and I encourage you to strive for things and experiences that are completely different from what I have. Nothing I've shared is intended to brag or boast, but I do want you to see that I'm really a genuinely happy person and that a life with scars can indeed be romantic.

A Romantic Life has Purpose

We often hear the saying, "things happen for a reason." You may or may not agree with that saying. As for me, I'm still searching for the answer. Can it be true? If each of our experiences happen for an enigmatic reason and there is a specific reason why we, you and I respectively, have to live with scars or disfigurement, and other people don't have to, I honestly don't know what that reason is—if there is one. I don't have the answer. It's inexplicable to me at this point. All I do know with absolute conviction is that this life with scars, yours and mine, can have a purpose if we want it to.

There is purpose in knowing where we come from. I have found purpose in understanding where I come from by appreciating past experiences. One thing that has been particularly helpful for me is the process of exploring and trying to understand the many challenges I have had to face with a visible difference. Living this way was the hardest thing for me growing up, but the accumulation of adversarial experiences, combined with good times, are what have shaped me into who I am. I find it fascinating that what started out as the catching of a common illness ended up turning into a lifetime of obstacles and priceless learning opportunities that will last with me forever. There has definitely been a purpose in realizing that.

My purpose of knowing where I come from: Because I was badly scarred by a serious case of chickenpox when I was six years old, I have been determined to succeed and reach my life goals while looking different from most people. I have had to push myself to keep a high self-esteem and maintain a positive outlook on life even when others didn't see me the same way. I have learned to use the challenges that come from having a physical difference in a positive way, for my own benefit, and by doing so my emotional and psychological well-being has prospered.

What is your purpose in knowing where you come from? What things have you learned along your way?

____

____

____

There is purpose in knowing what we are doing right now. The present is where we stand, and the decisions we make now determine a lot about our future. I know I cannot control everything, but make no mistake, being wise and prudent in the decisions I make right now will directly impact the overall person that I'll become later on.

The purpose in knowing what I am doing right now: Today I have what I consider to be a productive life overall. I try to find joy in the small things. I have a list of spiritual, financial, and temporal goals that I am working toward. I am happily married, and I am a father to multiple children. I am working hard, exercising my talents and set of skills to my best ability, and I am always continuing to learn new things. I have many weaknesses and problems to face every day, but I have the determination to conquer them all so that I might become a better and happier person as time continues.

What is the purpose in knowing what you're doing right now? Why are you doing those things?

____

____

____

There is purpose in knowing where we are going. If there is one thing I absolutely hate it's the feeling of being lost, and to a certain extent I can control whether I get lost or not. Like you, I have something called agency, which is the ability to be my own agent and act for myself. It is a very powerful gift, and one that none of us should overlook. With agency we can each choose a direction in which to go.

Knowing where we are going in life isn't merely about choosing a career or deciding where we are going to live. It isn't only about obtaining economic freedom or even independence. Knowing where we're going is also about knowing who we are becoming as a person and about creating behavior patterns for ourselves as we continue on. The real purpose in choosing a path of travel is to influence future environments in which we will live later on.

The purpose of knowing where I am going: I envision a bright future. Of course not everything will be perfect, but a lot of good can and will happen because of what I'm choosing to do now. I'm going to continue to bring these lessons to other people, particularly the lessons of living with scars and disfigurement. I'm going in this direction because I've already seen how these things can change lives, and changing lives for the better is what brings me the most joy.

What is the purpose in knowing where you are going? Why are you going in that direction?

____

____

____

____

A Romantic Life has Passion

Passion is what gives life its meaning; it refrains us from living monotonously and predictably and it removes the dull from a routine. Without passion life loses its flavor, authenticity, and intimacy. When we're passionate about something or someone, we become self-motivated because we feel good about what we're doing. Passion has no need of discipline or coercion because we're inspired to act passionately. When we're passionate we enjoy the engagement and presence of being and doing whatever it is we're involved with.

An example of my own passion can be characterized by the passionate relationship I have with my wife, Andrea. Back when we first met, I was in South America serving a mission for my church in the country of Uruguay. There were a thousand small things about her that caught my attention right away, but from the very start I had one overall feeling—she was the girl for me. I didn't exactly know why, but I knew it was true. It's incredible because although we're from different parts of the world and have different cultures and traditions, we're so very much the same. I saw our connection from the beginning and the impulse I had to be with her was so intuitive, it was passionate.

When we met, I also met the literal version of the girl of my dreams. I had always dreamt of finding a love like ours, one that's unconditional, self-driven, and exciting, but a part of me didn't think it was going to be possible. For a long time I doubted it, and my scars were one reason I had for doubting. I was overly self-conscious, and part of me didn't believe a beautiful girl like her would ever see past the surface. But then she came along and proved me wrong. Never once has she made me feel awkward about who I am or about what I look like. To the contrary, she constantly builds me up and makes me feel awesome. She has shown me that to her, nothing about my scars or appearance is strange or out of place; they are part of who I am. It's one thing to think those things on your own, but when the person you love has the same feelings, and when they love your scars even more than you do, it means the world. Andrea just happens to be infatuated with my scars, and yes, she is still the girl of my dreams.

Ever since our relationship began, I have been passionate about us and about what we have together. I'm so passionate that I'm willing to do anything and everything in order to be with her forever. In the beginning I went the distance. I sold everything I owned and traveled around the world twice before I could marry her. I worked three jobs, saved every penny, and fought through the legality of immigration in order to start our life together. There was a lot of risk involved, and it took a lot of sacrifice from both of us, but we did it passionately. We're together now, and everything it took for us to get here was well worth it.

I am to this day self-motivated to keep our relationship reinforced and unyielding to anything that would draw us apart. The love I have for her grows richer all the time, and our union is garrisoned by an effort to live romantically and passionately all the time.

Note: A life with passion does not require a romantic relationship to exist like the one I've described. You might not have a relationship like this yet, or you may not even want one. Each of us is different. This relationship is only one example of something that I am passionate about. It has been demonstrated by how I have sacrificed and risked everything for it. The passion that you have for something or for someone can be expressed differently.

When you have passion for something, you're dedicated to it, and so dedicated that you're willing to take risks and sacrifice what you already have for it. You're self-driven to it and enjoy with excitement whatever it is. Passion can be expressed for just about anything. To tell what you're passionate about, ask yourself what motivates you more than anything. What thrills you beyond any other activity? What do you care most about and would be willing to chase to the end of the earth for?

What are you passionate about?

____

____

____

____

What are you willing to risk or sacrifice for your passion?

____

____

____

____

How do you express passion?

____

____

____

____

A Romantic Life has Adventure

Romance of every kind is an adventure, and the excitement that comes from living adventurously should be felt by all of us. By trying new things and by going new distances we expose ourselves to an inspiriting and enlivening thrill. When we're adventurous we feel courageous, bold, and we get a taste of just how vigorous and alive we can be. This life with scars, just like any life, is too short and too precious to not incorporate the sensations of emotional enterprise regularly. So if you haven't lately, go ahead and make an opportunity for yourself to live a tremendous undertaking. It's time to be adventurous!

There are many ways to add more adventure to our lives. Some basic ideas include:

- Traveling to a place where you have never been before
- Tasting new food; experiencing a new culture
- Jumping on an intimidating opportunity, or...
- Doing something spontaneous and completely out of your ordinary routine.

Adventure comes through taking advantage of opportunistic activities, big and small. One evening when I was in my early twenties, I received a phone call that was totally out of the ordinary. It was a spontaneous call for adventure, extended to me from my closest friend. If you had known the two of us back then, you'd also know that we were practically inseparable. Best friends, the kind that makes every day an adventure together. That particular conversation, however, sparked one of the greatest adventures we would ever share.

"My friend called to ask if I would join him and his Dad in a flight to Mexico, in a private airplane, the very next morning, and embark on a long weekend fishing trip in the Sea of Cortez!"

The opportunity of going on a trip like that came out of nowhere! My jaw dropped at the sound of his spellbinding invitation. I think my heart even stopped! All of a sudden I found myself frozen by fortuity and perplexed by a dazzling sense of wonderment. Fly to Mexico in a private plane? Tomorrow? And go deep-sea fishing? It seemed too good to be true!

An adventure like that one was going to involve all of the ideas I just mentioned on how to create an adventure. If I went, I would be traveling to a place I had never been before. I would be tasting new food and experiencing a new culture. The opportunity was intimidating, for I had never flown in a private plane before, and it was spontaneous—completely out of the ordinary!

My initial response was enthusiastic, but clumsy at best. I was so excited to go that I started tripping over my own feet and began stuttering like a buffoon. "F...Fi...Fishing? ...i..in Mexico?..Fl...Flying?... Uhhhh....hahaha! Dude, what's going on," I yelled. "What are you even talking about?" I managed a few words before being swept away in awe and collapsing dumbstruck on the floor of my bedroom.

Quickly, I scrambled around for the phone and held it close while he relayed a breathtaking itinerary. We would be leaving the very next morning before the sun came up. Once at the airport we'd board a private plane, just four of us, and after arriving in Mexico we'd stay in a beach house right on the ocean's edge. We'd then have several days to go fishing!

After the invite concluded, my friend waited anxiously for an answer. Would I jump all over this rare chance to live adventurously, or would I come up with a ridiculously deficient excuse to not go? Still shocked and bewildered by surprise, my thoughts raced in all directions. Was I dreaming? Was this conversation even real? Had I actually been smacked in the face by a jewel opportunity? How? And why? There was no time to think it through completely. I had to make an instantaneous decision and respond right then and there.

Of course I went!

Early morning came quickly. We arrived at the airport, packed and ready to fly.

When the hanger door opened, to our great astonishment the airplane we saw waiting for us was unexpectedly much smaller in size than what either of us had imagined. It was really tiny! We were speechless. All we could do was look at the miniature aircraft and laugh hysterically. We hadn't even left yet, and due to this striking discovery our weekend excursion was already the biggest adventure we had ever had!

The airplane itself made the adventure worth remembering forever. I can tell you now that flying in a bird that small is the most fun way of traveling that I have ever experienced. It had a single propeller in front and just enough room inside for our four bodies and some fishing poles. It was such a small aircraft that when we flew, I remember having the exuberant feeling that we were being tossed about by the elements of space. And I remember how I felt as I peered out through a little window towards the earth below me. As I watched the landscape below, passing over the desert landscapes of Southern Utah, Arizona, and making our way towards the Gulf of California into Mexico, the feeling of being alive was incredible. The thrill and excitement of adventure was so indescribably big that for some reason, unbeknown to me, I felt like the luckiest guy alive.

I could go on and on in telling you all about that vacation. After all, it's one of my favorite stories. The airplane ride was only the beginning. I would love to tell you about the things we did in Mexico. I could describe to you the peaceful ambiance of the beach house, or expound on what it’s like to be in a boat overflowing with fish. I could try to explain the jubilant sensation of riding a Jeep along the sandy coastline, or of watching enormous flocks of seagulls circle around a colorful and prismatic sunset. I wish I could paint to you the sound of waves crashing beneath us while we slept on the upstairs deck of the house. I'd tell you about the stores, friendly people at the street markets, and the flavor of native shrimp tacos. Instead, I'm going to save that conversation for another time.

There is one main point that I want to get across by this narrative, and that is *adventure*. Adventure of any kind, big or small, adds life to the one we're living. Had I not taken advantage of the opportunity when it came to me, none of those experiences would have happened; none of those memories would exist.

Make Adventure Happen

Sometimes adventure comes to us, but other times we have to get proactive and make adventure happen on our own, or it won't. Sometimes we accept opportunities, and other times we make them for ourselves.

We all naturally want to enjoy life and get the most out of it while we can. If adventure is absent, then our rhythm of routine can become bland. Life can lose its potency. It can become stale and the energy keeping us afloat can get lost if we don't take care of it creatively. If at any time you get worried that you're not getting enough enjoyment out of life, its presumably time to get proactive and add some adventure. If opportunities aren't coming to you, then make them happen on your own. Go somewhere. Do something. Live.

A morsel of adventure goes a long way! Don't be convinced that you have to go on an exotic cruise to the Bahamas or climb Mount Everest in order to change your life. Start small. Remain in your budget. By doing something new or out of the ordinary you'll be off to a great adventurous start.

In your words, why is it important to live adventurously?

____

____

____

____

____

____

Describe a life without adventure.

____

____

____

____

____

How can you add more adventure to your life right now?

____

____

____

____

____

____

A Romantic Life is a Life of Devotion

Devotion is the synthesis of having loyalty, love, and passion. It is the synchronization of our dedication, discipline, and enthusiasm. When we are devoted to something we give our whole soul to it and we consecrate ourselves for its cause.

This final quality will be separated into two parts. The first part is our devotion to our own self, our well-being and state of affairs. The latter part focuses on our outward devotion to others. We need both parts in order to fully maximize our potential and reap the best fruits out of life.

Devotion for Self

As you've found, this course has concentrated on the importance of making you aware of the value of your life and of the true value of your scars. Lessons have been taught about how you can improve yourself individually, emotionally and cognitively. You've learned how some of your greatest challenges can serve to make you strong if you choose to allow them to.

A pivotal question: Why should you be strong and overcome life's challenges if life is ultimately going to end with death and is temporary?

Over the years this has been a recurrently asked question. Typically, the individual asking is seriously wondering why they should be strong, or what the point is of overcoming their challenges. Normally, the person is passing through a stage of depression. Their question, well worth answering, is always answered with another.

My answer: Death will surely come, and because neither of us can prove what happens afterwards, what will you do to vanguard your remaining time and take charge of the life you have left?

All of us who are alive will eventually die, and one person's life is just as fragile as the next one’s. Each of our lives also shares the same living potential. Each of us can potentially pursue happiness or misery between now and the time of death. Our circumstances might vary, but potentially we are all equal in this respect.

So my question for you is, what will you do for yourself to pursue happiness over misery during the time you have left to live? How will you vanguard your time and take charge of your life? The scars that you carry can serve for your good or they can serve you poorly. It is up to you.

I've learned something for myself that helps answer this question, and it has to do with a thing called devotion.

Be devoted to yourself.
Be devoted to yourself and to the life that you have by being loyal to yourself. Have passion for your own well-being and a love for the fact that you can live and make something out of your life now and today.

Self-devotion does not refer to a state of pride or self-centeredness. It isn't about being mindless or ravenous until the end. Self-devotion recognizes that to be someone who is useful to others and happy with your own life, the self has to first be balanced and productive. Priorities and life objectives have to be in check. Self-discipline and dedication to reaching worthwhile goals are what should drive you forward, and you should have enthusiasm for things to come.

If we aren't devoted to ourselves and to our own growth, we cannot show devotion by our own example to anyone else.

This course is a tool that you can use in self-devotion.

The lessons and principles contained in this course are entirely for you. This has not been a mandatory guide; it is a self-help guide and one that you can repeat, utilize, or enucleate as often and as much as you wish. It has always been my desire, even before I began compiling and writing it, that you can find a way to use its contents to find clarity to the life with scars that you have to live. I hope it has helped you in some way.

How has this course helped you to have a better outlook on life?

____

____

____

____

____

____

Devotion to Others

As you continue on your journey through life, remember that you carry something with you of unspeakable value—a story. And yours is not just any story. Yours is a survival story, a story of overcoming great odds.

There are others; in fact, there is a vast population of individuals out there who are, right now, in this very moment, gravely challenged with scars of their own. These individuals believe that their scars or disfigurement or other visible difference is a roadblock hindering their potential of being who they want to become in life. They feel betrayed or broken by the mere happenstance of living. They don't see their differences as visible or invisible tokens of experience, and they don't treat them as if they were emblems of a past full of priceless lessons and learning opportunities. They don't use their scars for their own good.

And why?

They simply haven't reached that point yet.

But you and I can help them. If this course has helped you in any way, please reach out and share what you've learned with another. Pass it on. Share your knowledge and happiness with someone else. If and when you do, you'll discover one of life's greatest gifts—the joy that comes from giving and from devoting yourself to others.

After sharing a portion or this entire course with someone else, describe the experience. What did they learn? What did you learn?

____

____

____

____

____

____

Conclusion

A life with scars was never intended to be an easy one and no one would ever confess that it is. No. A life with scars is difficult and the challenges we face are comprehensive. But this life with scars that we're living is definitely worth it.

You can build a romantic life for yourself by incorporating the qualities spoken about in this section to the way you conduct your day. First, find purpose. Find purpose in what you've been through and in the places that you've been. Discover purpose in what you're doing and in where you're going. Next, have passion. Be passionate about what you do and be passionate to the people in your life who matter most. Then be adventurous. Feel the vigor and thrill of being alive by accepting and creating adventures for yourself. Finally, be devoted to yourself and to others. Seek the best conditions for your own well-being, and in turn, share what you know with other people in need. As each of these qualities is added to the composition of your daily behavior, a romantic life will be sown.

Like me, you are a *rare case* living a life with scars.

I have an idea for both of us...

Let's each become a *rare case* of purpose,

A *rare case* of passion, a *rare case* of adventure.

Let's, each of us, become a *rare case* of devotion.

Let's make the best we can out of this life, and let's begin right now.

Photography Credits

Clayton Hall, photographer, began his career specializing in Fashion & Beauty and Portraiture at Clayton Hall Photographic Studios, New York, NY (1979 to 1994). His work has appeared on both the covers and pages of many leading magazines including: Accessories Magazine, ASMP/AZ, BOMA/New York, Fender Frontline, Flair, Leaders Magazine, Manhattan Catalog, Phoenix Magazine, Rolling Stone, Vogue Health & Beauty, W's Accessories, Woman's Day Health & Beauty, and Women's Wear Daily. In 1994, Hall moved west and opened Empire West Studios in Tempe, AZ. It was at Empire West Studios that Hall developed a unique working method for models and talent (children, teens and adults) looking to break into the fashion and entertainment industries. The basis for Hall's specialty is "Performance Photography," a studio based style of shooting which emphasizes the sitter's movement and expression. Whether photographing portraits, fashion, beauty, models or talent, Hall's style of shooting has resulted in great success for many clients. For further information on Clayton Hall and to see samples of his work, visit www.EmpireWestStudios.com; 480-303-9359; (ch@empireweststudios.com). Mr. Hall's photo above by Barbara E. Muller. Clayton's photographs appear in this book on pages 7, 11, 55, 80, 138, and 154.

Claudia Traversa, Photographer, has had a growing international following since 2008 for her unique talent of capturing human emotions and interactions in their natural forms. Born and living in Uruguay, her reputation has been largely recognized through various channels of social media, which have carried her works abroad. She specializes in commercial and non-commercial photography. For more information, visit www.claudiatraversa.com. Claudia's photographs appear in this book on pages 28, 34, 43, 45, 60, 63, 77, 85, 87, 109, and 121.